Invitational Ministry

Invitational Ministry

MOVE YOUR CHURCH
from
Membership
to Discipleship

Laurene Beth Bowers

CHALICE
PRESS
ST. LOUIS, MISSOURI

All Scripture quotations, unless otherwise indicated, are from The Holy Bible, English Standard Version® (ESV®), copyright © 2001 by Crossway, a publishing ministry of Good News Publishers. Used by permission. All rights reserved.

Scripture quotations marked (NIV) are taken from the HOLY BIBLE, NEW INTERNATIONAL VERSION®. NIV®. Copyright © 1973, 1978, 1984 by International Bible Society. Used by permission of Zondervan Publishing House. All rights reserved.

Cover image: BigStock photo

Cover design: Elizabeth Wright

www.chalicepress.com

Print: 9780827216655

EPUB: 9780827216662   EPDF: 9780827216679

10 9 8 7 6 5 4 3 2 1   13   14   15   16   17   18

Library of Congress Cataloging-in-Publication Data available upon request

Printed in the United States of America

With love to my sisters and brother,
Sharon Lynn (Bowers) Grossman,
Marna Robin (Bowers) Orcutt
Kyle Robert Bowers

Contents

Foreword

For over four decades the congregations of what was once called the Protestant mainline have been wailing and gnashing their teeth over an accelerating decline in numbers, energy, and resources. The presentation of sobering data about decreases in membership and financial support has become an annual ritual at most judicatory meetings. This downward trajectory is no historical accident, for it is rooted in multiple dynamics that run deep within the history of Christianity in America. Primary among them has been the unfortunate legacy of the mainline's unofficial (and sometimes official) cultural establishment. Since colonial days, the churches of the mainline have tacitly assumed that individuals would naturally want to affiliate with them because membership in a Congregational, Presbyterian, Episcopal, etc. congregation would bring with it enhanced status, social influence, and the satisfaction of being part of the dominant cultural sensibility. It was assumed that people would join and remain within the fold out of loyalty, tribalism, or a vague sense of the propriety of belonging to venerable organizations that provided the nation's sacred canopy. Absolutely contrary to the mainline's instincts was the notion that a compelling case would need to made to persuade people to get up early on a Sunday morning and attend one of their worship services. After decades of experimentation with various strategies of evangelism and church growth, the mainline has still not discovered a way to overcome its heritage of evangelistic inertia.

Some of the more recent strategies to attract the never churched and the formerly churched have not been particularly successful. Often the failure is due to the fact that the "case" made for joining a mainline congregation simply offers benefits and services that can easily be had elsewhere, without the inconvenience of contributing to an annual stewardship campaign. For example, the promise of "friendship" has often been the chief enticement. But if someone really longs for friendship, it is obvious these days that sociability and even genuine support can be found in a host of secular organizations and informal affiliative networks. An individual need not join a mainline congregation to find friends; often a local club will do quite nicely. Similarly, if someone needs help dealing with the tribulations of daily life, secular therapists, often highly trained and affordable ones, are readily available. The mainline pastor is not the only counseling show in town.

Moreover, blandishing the virtues of a belief system with precise boundaries and definitive answers has not been any more successful than promising friends or therapy. In postmodern culture, more and more individuals have become quite comfortable with exploring and entertaining multiple perspectives simultaneously. Recent generations have learned to be restive with any institution's claim to possess unadulterated truth. Consequently, the prospect of a theologically homogenous religious community with a uniform doctrine is not particularly alluring. Folks are increasingly sensitive to the fact that religious convictions are at least partly the fruits of diverse social locations, idiosyncratic personal dynamics, and exposure to particular traditions. It has becomes evident that the differences in spiritual yearnings and drives among human beings are deep and genuine. As a result, the prospect of a one-size-fits-all theology or spirituality seems off-putting to many of our contemporaries.

So, what can a church offer to the world that no other organization can? If it is neither friendship nor orthodoxy, what could it be? In this volume, Laurene Bowers proposes a novel possibility. What if the one thing that a church can provide is an opportunity for individuals to share and explore the significance of their perhaps very faintly experienced spiritual aspirations? What if unchurched individuals were invited to probe questions of ultimate meaning with those who are already part of the congregation? What if this conversation could be fostered in the context of a community that cares passionately about matters of ultimate concern and is not afraid to talk about them? In Laurene Bowers' pages the contours of such an "invitational ministry" are attractively limned.

Invitational ministry emerges as the extension of a heartfelt offer to those beyond the walls of the church to participate in a candid conversation about the hopes, fears, longings, and satisfactions that constitute personal faith. This invitational ministry would not be the imposition of an ideological agenda or an induction into a normative worship style. Rather, it would be the honest cultivation of empathic spiritual relationships and a commitment among the churched and the unchurched to engage in continuing mutual religious support.

It just may be that the prospect of the sharing of multiple vantage points on God, life, death, and everything in-between could stir the hearts and capture the imaginations of the unchurched. It just may be that this strategy could tap into the spiritual ferment that characterizes our era and inject new vigor into the mainline. It just may be that the cross-fertilization of the churched and the unchurched could enable a multidimensional, fully orbed gospel to emerge with new depth and richness.

Lee Barrett
Henry and Mary Stager Professor of Theology
Lancaster Theological Seminary

Preface

These are challenging times for mainline Christianity. Yet they are also times filled with opportunities to become a new kind of church, relevant for a new day and age. One of the most significant challenges at the present time is to remain hopeful.[1] Hope conveys that we have faith in Jesus, his disciples, and the community around us. Hope inspires people to be generous with their energy and talent. It encourages people to take risks; to try new things with the expectation of achieving different results. Hope generates creativity and innovation. Hopeful people are more likely to invite others to church because they can witness to how the church provides a forum for them to share their experiences and form their faith in new and exciting ways. I pray that the reader will embrace such hope while reading this book.

When we do not feel hopeful, we become anxious, and, when anxious, we look back to a time in the past when we felt less anxious. Church members recall "the glory days" when the pews were filled with young families eagerly anticipating a new year of Sunday school. As long as a congregation was "warm and friendly" toward visitors, those visitors would return the following Sunday. Members often left money to the church in their wills to sustain its ministries long after they went to heaven to be with Jesus. Life in the church was good!

But as it did to Lot's wife, looking back can turn us into pillars of salt or, in more contemporary imagery, columns of granite. Frozen with fear, we don't explore our options because we can't imagine any new possibilities. Instead, we invest our limited energy in sustaining "the way we have always done things" under the premise that the way of doing church in 1960 should still work in 2013. The way we "did" church worked in 1960 and was positively reinforced by attracting that generation of believers. Because it worked, it became etched in stone as the way the next generation should also want to do church. However, today the current generation of young people is looking for different ways to form their faith. Just thinking about what that "something different" might look like makes those of us in older generations anxious, but it should not prevent us from reaching out to the next generation and inviting them to participate in this process of change.

Wilderness wanderings can be spiritual experiences. We can't go back! No one wants to join an organization whose best days are behind it. The days are gone when people come to church to watch the pastor do the ministry; the days are upon us when we will create learning environments to teach ministers new skills for Christian practices such as caring, hospitality, and invitation. The young generation is searching for faith communities that are nonjudgmental so that they can talk about their faith and share their own stories. People come to church hoping for these experiences, not to be asked to serve on a committee for the rest of their natural lives!

As a pastor for twenty-seven years, I served four congregations in New England as we made the transition from glorifying the past to being excited about the future. As the pastor, *I* did not numerically grow any of these congregations, but I did empower the members to become disciples. These congregations came to genuinely believe that God was (and is) calling them to a new ministry: one of invitation. They turned to me, the minister, to teach and equip them. While I expect that many of the readers of this book will be clergy, I hope that other congregational leaders will also feel called to lead their congregations in these efforts. Whereas the pastor's job is to provide opportunities for faith formation and identify practices that facilitate this process, it is the responsibility of every believer in Jesus to become his disciple and to reach out to those who are unchurched.*

As the Conference Associate Minister of Congregational Life and Vitality for the Penn Central Conference, United Church of

---

* Throughout this book, I will refer to those who do not attend church as "the unchurched." I make this disclaimer because although this word presents a viewpoint from "within," it seems less accurate to use the other popular term "seeker" when not all of the unchurched are seeking anything from a religious organization. I struggled for some time to come up with a better word, but in the final editing, decided that it was the most descriptive when addressing an audience of people who are "churched."

Christ, I felt called to cast this vision, not just for one church, but for many who are in the process of discerning new ministries. I strive to balance being prophetic with creating a sense of urgency; helping congregations identify their current strengths, emphasize those strengths, and resource one another to build one another up. I consult with congregations on an ongoing basis, teach in the Road to Vitality program, and recently designed a program called The Ezekiel Project to help congregations through a self-assessment process. The congregations here are responding well to these efforts and are beginning to reap the benefits of reconnecting with their neighborhoods.

I wish to convey a word of thanks to all those with whom I share my daily ministry here at the Penn Central Conference: to Marja Coons-Torn, the Conference Minister; Thom Webster, Conference Associate Minister of Pastoral Leadership and Discernment; Bruce Druckenmiller, Conference Associate Minister of Outdoor Ministries, Youth, and Young Adults; Brenda Waleff, Commissioned Minister of Communications; Wendy Hepler, Administrative Assistant; and Janice Mountain, Profile Coordinator. I thank all of the pastors in this conference who have been so welcoming. We truly work together as a team committed to helping our congregations to spiritually and numerically grow. Many thanks to Lee Barrett, Mary B. and Henry P. Stager Chair in Theology and Professor of Systematic Theology at Lancaster Theological Seminary, with whom I co-taught a course on Invitational Ministry this past summer. I also wish to thank my husband of thirty years, Kent William Rhodehamel and my children, Christian, Kyle, and Kelyne.

Introduction

I begin this book with three confessions. First, I admit that every time I stood at the pulpit and said, "Invite your friends and family to worship next Sunday," I knew it was unlikely that anyone would actually do so. Members would look at me as if to say, "Surely you aren't speaking to me!" Regretfully, I continued this ritual week after week, month after month, expecting that, one day, lightning would strike and some great program or special worship service would inspire every member to invite an unchurched person to attend. Eventually something did change: my level of frustration with the congregation and, I suspect, their level of frustration with me. I was trying to get them to do something that they were unequipped to do. I confess that it has taken me a long time to realize that the problem was not with the members. The problem stemmed from my leadership. I needed to learn to equip them with the skills to practice invitational ministry.

Just as pastors often hold the unrealistic expectation that members will suddenly begin inviting others to church, so do members hold on to the unrealistic expectation that suddenly the unchurched will show up at their front door. Members concede, "We just have to manage through this time of scarcity until the day when the mass of the American public will see the light and be motivated to attend church." The phenomenon of mainline decline is perceived as a societal problem, therefore beyond the control and responsibility of the local congregation. Given the perception that the problem is outside of organized religion, members assume that the solution will also come from beyond its walls. Perhaps an upswing in the economy or a national crisis will suddenly motivate those who've left church to return, and those who have never participated in church to show interest. As long as congregations perceive that they didn't cause the problem and can't solve it, they are left feeling helpless.

When members of religious organizations feel this way, they tend to over-control that which lies within their realm—that is, the internal functions within the church. This gives them something to do while they patiently wait for the masses to appear. Inwardly focused, their conversations revolve around the woes of the organization. These conversations, in turn, make them feel anxious, even desperate, fearing that if something doesn't change soon "out there," their beloved organization will cease to exist. To manage their anxiety, they default to a self-serving mission statement, such as, "We should take care of our own." The working premise is, "It is better to take care of ourselves before we take care of others." As they invest energy in self-care, they lose interest in the needs of the community around them. Meanwhile, the community views the church as a private club, with the purpose of caring for those who join and pay an annual pledge.

My second confession is that, for a long time, I did not do my share of inviting anyone either. My everyday interactions were with members of the congregation. Those in positions of power within the church expected me to focus on the people who had already become believers in Jesus, not those out in the community struggling to find their faith. I enabled the congregation's inward focus by doing my best to "take care" of those who had engaged my pastoral services and paid my salary. I prided myself on being their beloved pastor. If, by some miracle I was able to do everything that everyone expected from me and found myself with extra time, only then could I turn my attention to ministering in the community. But I never seemed to find that time.

I led by example, focusing my energy inward, and the congregation followed quite well. I didn't invite anyone to church and neither did they. I thought it was their job to invite others and numerically grow the congregation, and they thought it was mine. There was even talk about my getting a pay raise if more people start coming (and pledging). For a while, I bought into by this expectation, but soon realized that, single-handedly, I could not numerically grow a congregation. We began pointing fingers at who was to blame for our current predicament, which easily might have sparked a wildfire of conflict. I glided safely along by maintaining my beloved status, working to please the people who would come to my defense. As long as I could remain well-liked by the majority, I didn't have much incentive to take risks and introduce the idea of doing church differently.

My third confession is that I really didn't want to know why people weren't coming to church. What I feared was that people weren't coming because, as the worship leader, I wasn't providing a meaningful experience. What if members weren't inviting others because worship was boring and irrelevant? I displaced my fear with the excuse that I didn't have enough freedom to be creative in worship, and so any boredom was a result of having to fit my style into a preset liturgical mold. Afraid that I was to blame because members were not inviting others to church, I shifted the focus onto the members and away from myself.

The Turning Point

The turning point came when I was asked to visit a family in the neighborhood who had recently experienced a tragedy and was struggling to make sense of it. After I prayed for and with them, I invited them to church on Sunday. This wasn't my usual practice; I surprised even myself by extending the invitation. The couple looked at each other and said, "Thank you. No one has ever invited us to church before. When we moved into this neighborhood, we kept hoping that someone would invite us. We need church now more than ever." They attended the following Sunday and the congregation embraced them warmly. Later, when asked to share their testimony during worship, they spoke of how God had given them the strength to cope with their crisis by bringing them into that community of faith. Since then, they have invited others in the community who had also experienced tragedy.

Gradually the conversation within the church shifted away from our internal burdens to wondering if there were others outside our walls in need of a Christian community. We became increasingly aware of how many people were struggling with issues related to daily living. We had always assumed that people in the neighborhood were relatively happy, content with their relationships and with finding spiritual formation on their own. When we began to reach out and listen intently to their stories— stories often filled with pain, suffering, and misery—we realized that we had not only let the community down, we had let Jesus down. Jesus calls us to minister to those experiencing sorrow, sadness, and depression. We weren't equipping people to do ministry, and they were getting bored in their role as care-receivers. I finally realized that the best way to take care of members is to equip them for the ministry of changing others' lives. In this process, their own lives are changed as well.

I asked God what needed to change within me to lead a congregation in this outward-focused mission, and I discerned that I needed to acquire new leadership skills. As I changed my leadership strategy, church members became "disciples"–called to fulfill Jesus' commission to make disciples of others. The more I believed that God was calling us to reach out to the unchurched, the more the congregation came to believe it. The more enthusiastic I was to do ministry in the neighborhood, the more the congregation got excited about building relationships with people they didn't yet know. The more I led by example by inviting others, the more the disciples in the congregation did likewise. Instead of working to sustain a private country club culture in which membership required paying dues and showing up periodically, the church began practicing invitational ministry as the core of its identity.

We had previously been functioning like Noah's Ark, drifting along in a building so tightly locked up that it prevented us from hearing the cries of the people drowning around us. When God sent an olive branch, we opened the window to receive it and searched for dry, fertile land for our new ministry. We stopped asking people to come so that we could increase our membership, and, instead, offered learning opportunities for people to become ministers who were prepared to swim in turbulent waters. Once again, the church had a purpose and the members were excited. The accompanying numerical growth was only an indicator that Jesus' disciples were now practicing invitational ministry.

This book offers practical strategies to transform a congregation from being members of a church to becoming disciples for Jesus and practicing invitational ministry. I believe this is the most effective approach to turn the decline around and grow a congregation numerically. Together, we'll explore the reasons members do not feel comfortable inviting others; why they feel like they don't know what to say; and how to help them overcome the idea that "evangelism" must be pushy and persuasive. Disciples will be able to learn new skills so that their adult children will come to church and bring their grandchildren. I will discuss how to offer an invitation, what to invite people to, and how to create a culture of invitation within the congregation. I invite you to join me as we walk through this process.

Chapter 1

The Christian Practice of Invitational Ministry

Recently the quest to revitalize the church has turned to the renewal of Christian practices. Diana Butler Bass observes that congregations engaged in Christian practices such as prayer, hospitality, and invitation are the ones experiencing revitalization.[2] All three practices work together to make disciples and produce numerical church growth. Once people are invited and show interest by coming to the church, they should be warmly received through the practice of hospitality. Similarly, practicing invitation and hospitality without prayer may numerically grow a congregation quickly, but prayer is foundational to spiritual formation. Without it, new people will drift away as quickly as they appeared. Invitation, hospitality, and prayer are three important practices for disciple-making

The mainline church has a well-established tradition of practicing prayer and hospitality. One of the reasons members say they come to church is to share joys and concerns by requesting prayers and lighting candles. They engage in this practice because they believe in the power of praying within a faith community. With respect to hospitality, almost all congregations describe themselves as "warm and friendly." The hope is that when visitors attend, they will feel welcome and if they feel welcome, they will return the following Sunday. When a visitor does return, those who welcomed them initially now feel affirmed for their hospitality skills. Thus, members of any congregation, whether declining or growing, have opportunities to practice hospitality and prayer.

But what distinguishes a congregation in decline from one that is numerically growing is the addition of invitational ministry to these core Christian practices. Unlike prayer and hospitality, the mainline church has almost no longstanding practice of inviting others to come to church. Historically, members were baptized into the congregation and remained faithful to it for the rest of their lives. If they moved, they sought out a new church that was denominationally affiliated with their former church. People died, but more people were born, replenishing the supply of members. Congregations could depend on the cycle of life for their sustenance, and invitational ministry was not a needful practice.

Affiliating with a church out of a sense of obligation does not carry the weight it did in former years. Today, going to church is not socially expected. (For instance, how many employers allow Sundays off?) Many people still believe in God, but they may refer to themselves as "spiritual but not religious." Young people do not have the same need to belong to organizations to define their identity.[3] They do not see how a religious organization can help them to form their spirituality, when there are other avenues such as yoga and meditation. Those who attend church have not articulated what the church has to offer, and so it appears irrelevant and outdated. They have often not invited the unchurched, and so they can't tell if the uninvited are even interested. The unchurched often express it this way: "I don't know anyone who goes to church, so I can't really say if I would want to go. No one has invited me."

Those who were brought up attending church and remained members through adulthood have not had to think about why they attend. One of the most cited reasons is obligation: "I was baptized into this church and so I continue to come to support its ministries." But those who were not raised in the church do not feel this same sense of obligation. Among them, to think about attending is a choice—based on a set of good reasons. Those who are obligated don't know what those other reasons might be: "I've never really thought about why I go to church, I just go because I have always gone." These people are ill-equipped to help others discern the reasons why someone who has not always attended would decide to do so.

Why Go to Church?

Invitational ministry seeks to help the unchurched identify the "why." First, we need to help them discern their own interests and spiritual needs, and then assess whether or not the church is in a position to meet those interests and needs. Church members assume that what meets their own spiritual needs should meet everyone else's spiritual needs regardless of age, ethnicity, economic background, or other cultural factors. Some members don't even know what their own needs are, never mind someone else's, especially someone with no experience in being part of a religious organization. Lack of awareness is a major stumbling block and can undermine efforts to numerically grow a congregation. To help another person answer the "why" question, members first need to be able to answer it themselves.

Experiencing God at Church

Many members will say they attend church to have a spiritual experience: "I go to church to be with God." The sanctuary evokes a sense of sacred awe as the believer encounters the mysterious. In worship, the focus is on deepening one's connectedness with God through music, ritual, scripture, and the sermon. From the perspective of the churched, worship is a spiritual experience that takes place within a religious organization. Jesus promises his presence when two or three are gathered in his name. Believers gather to experience the presence of God in Jesus Christ, within the context of the religious community.

Those who don't go to church report that they experience God in other settings. They may experience God while hiking up a mountain, kayaking on a lake, or sitting in their backyard. They feel a special affinity for nature and reflect upon how its beauty connects them to their sacred selves. By using meditation practices from Eastern religions such as Buddhism, they may find inner peace, serenity, and tranquility. Integrating the mind, body, and spirit, they experience God in a yoga position or resting the mind in a quiet place. They don't feel the need to adhere to the tenets of one religion at the exclusion of another, and they like the freedom to experiment with a variety of religious practices. To have to fit one's spirituality into a specific religion seems confining and oppressive. As long as one is "spiritual but not religious" one does not have to narrow one's choices to subscribe to a particular religion.

The unchurched don't doubt that some people experience God in a worship service. They see going to worship as one option among many for connecting with God. If Sunday happens to be their only day of the week to catch up on sleep, it doesn't seem to make sense to fit that experience of God into an early hour. Some have heard church members claim that the only place to experience God is in a religious community, but they believe otherwise. When they are invited to a worship service, they will often respond, "If all the church has to offer me is an experience of God, I can experience God in a peaceful meadow." They don't feel the need to go to church to spend time with God.

Congregations that are making disciples do not invite people to church for the sole purpose of experiencing God. They gather to talk about their experiences of God, not only in the worship space, but in other settings as well. In small groups, members share how they encounter God in their daily lives, in their joys and struggles—witnessing to each other how they believe God is involved. Talking about these experiences helps people to understand God in new ways and from new perspectives, so that they are more in touch with God's activity and intervention. These sacred conversations help them with the process of forming and reforming their faith. New encounters summon believers to integrate these experiences into a coherent whole that encircles all that they believe.

Sharing Experiences of God Not Easy for All

This level of personal sharing does not come easily to some church members, especially those who have been raised with the adage, "Family problems stay in the family." Faith, for some, feels like a private matter between themselves and God. Creeds are read and affirmations of faith are recited to help the community verbalize what they believe (or are supposed to believe). Faith-sharing has become confined to the setting of worship. But today, congregational cultures that do not support faith-sharing, both within and outside of the context of a worship service, are destined for irrelevancy. If financial institutions never talked about finances and political organizations never talked politics, where would they be? And yet religious communities are often not talking about faith or spiritual matters. Those who are willing to feel discomfort will be those who become invitational ministers. They will learn how to manage their anxiety when talking about their faith so that they can witness to how they have spiritually benefited by attending church.

To manage the uneasiness in talking about faith, some congregations want to depend on the pastor, who is well-educated and is supposed to be knowledgeable about everything religious. Thus, according to some, the pastor should be the (only) one speaking about his or her experience of God. Pastors themselves may not feel comfortable sharing their *personal* experience of God. They have been trained to rely more heavily on the traditional doctrines held by the church to be sacrosanct. These concepts often delineate the boundary between what is believed in that religion/faith/denomination and what is "counter-belief." (The more technical term is "heresy.") Members who disagree with their pastor's theology usually keep that to themselves. The culture of the church supports the pastor as the all-knowing figure, and takes for granted the notion that the members are the ones to be filled with his or her wisdom and knowledge.

Friendships at Church

Members also say they attend a certain church because "that is where all my friends go to church." They cherish their long-term relationships with other members. These friendships encourage loyalty to a particular congregation: "I continue to go to this church because of the people." These friendships have been developed over time, as members support and care for one another through joys and sorrows. Often, the sense of loyalty extends to the pastor as well, especially if he or she has been their pastor for many years. Members also say they continue to attend because of their pastor's personality and/or preaching style. Friendships among members and liking the pastor are among the primary reasons why a current member attends one church and not another.

An invitation that offers friendship to someone not currently attending church, however, may receive a response such as, "If all the church has to offer me is friendship, I have enough friends." So how is friendship within a religious community different? The church is not merely a social organization, designed to offer friendship; instead, you need to reframe how you describe the relationships within the congregation. Those who attend the same church are "brothers and sisters in Christ," and, if so, then they are called to witness to one another by sharing their faith. I might not reveal to my friends outside the church what is going on in my life, while with my brothers and sisters I share these intimate details because I know that they will pray for me.

What Is Invitational Ministry?

Invitational ministry is a witness to one's faith and how that faith is being formed through the Christian practices embraced by the congregation (as well as the wider church). It answers the question, "Why do I go to church?" and identifies the various purposes of the organization.

Furthermore, invitational ministry seeks to answer the question, "Why is the church reaching out to the unchurched at this time?" This reason needs to be articulated as a theological statement. Invitational ministry requires a set of skills that every disciple can acquire with practice. Within mainline Protestant denominations, it is a relatively new practice and promises to become one of the most important ministries of this century. The most prevalent factor that distinguishes congregations that are numerically growing from those that are not is the practice of invitational ministry by members transitioning to be disciples.

Invitational ministry should be taught to every member of the congregation. It should not be delegated to a select few whose outgoing personalities seem to make it easier for them to invite others. Invitational ministry should not be assigned to an outreach or evangelism committee to be discussed, debated, and then shelved as a good intention, with no follow-through. Disciples embody a wide range of ministries, but a core value attached to these ministries is to make disciples of others. That process begins when one disciple invites another person to join them on the journey. When we reach a time when every member invites others to grow in faith through Christian practice, the church will be a different place than it is today. The prophesy that we are in the midst of a transformation or reawakening that the church goes through every five hundred years[4] will only be realized when we invite the unchurched and churched to get together and envision what that transformation will look like.

While a simple invitation, e.g., "Would you like to come to church with me?" is sometimes effective, as we saw in the last chapter, generally it is no longer an effective way to create interest. People not involved in church want to know how they will spiritually benefit by becoming part of a faith community. Simply inviting someone might have worked in a cultural environment in which everyone went to church, but, in contemporary times, we need to identify what the church has to offer in order to create interest and share our faith. Most members in mainline religion do not feel comfortable sharing their faith or inviting others to church. This presents a challenge. The "Unbinding" series by Martha Grace Reece is a good resource, consisting of four engaging books, designed to help members learn how to articulate their faith. These books can be used in sequence to help members learn how to share faith as an invitation.[5]

Another recommendation is to invite people to special events, rather than worship. Many church people have already tried to invite friends and family to a worship service (which is usually the destination intended by the question, "Do you want to come to church with me?"). Invitational events are planned to create interest among people who don't attend church, with particular attention to what will make them feel comfortable in developing relationships with people within the church. Through these relationships, members can discern what others' spiritual needs may be so that they can either change worship to meet those needs or help these visitors connect with another congregation who is willing to do so. An alternative way of thinking about it is that members are on a mission to answer the questions, "What ways to form faith (practices) might interest people? Which of those might our organization be able to offer?" However, people might not know what would interest them, and so the questions should not be posed directly. Invitational events and the relationships they encourage provide a forum for this discernment.

Invitational Ministry vs. Evangelism

In *Designing Contemporary Congregation,* I wrote about what I referred to at the time as "invitational evangelism."[6] In my more recent thinking, I have distanced myself from the concept of evangelism. I have done this for two reasons. First, in mainline

Protestantism, the word *evangelism* makes many people uncomfortable. Offering a course on evangelism in a congregation is likely to attract just a few takers, if any. The word conjures up images that heighten anxiety, such as going door to door trying to convince neighbors that if they don't go to church, they will go to hell. Congregation members themselves may have received such a knock on the door and recall feeling annoyed. Evangelism makes them think of people who are pushy, aggressive, and fanatical about their faith.

Second, and more importantly, I have distanced myself from the concept of evangelism because I am proposing a different approach. Evangelism seeks to make a change in the person being evangelized, not the person doing the evangelizing. Most of us can sense when someone is on a mission to change us. We build walls of resistance to keep that person from pushing his or her agenda upon us. Instead, invitational ministry seeks to help people identify their spiritual needs, and articulates how participating in congregational life can help meet those needs. The emphasis is on how the person will spiritually benefit.

Another difference is that evangelism attempts to move persons from the comfort of experiencing God in the backyard to the discomfort of an unfamiliar setting (a religious organization). They experience God while sitting by the seashore listening to the waves. Think about it from their perspective: Why would they want to exchange the seashore for a formal place with hard pews, convoluted symbols, and confusing rituals? Invitational ministry agrees that we can experience God outside of the church; in fact, seeking these experiences is encouraged. But only in a faith community can we have a conversation about those experiences, and such conversation facilitates the formation of faith. As individuals share their experiences with others, we learn from one another the many ways that God is actively involved in our lives.

Another difference between evangelism and invitational ministry is that invitational ministers attempt to imagine what it is like not to be a part of a church and respond accordingly, in order to anticipate possible questions:

What happens in a worship service and what am I supposed to do?

Why do you _____ (fill in with any of a dozen things: "stand to pray," "take an offering," "drink wine [or juice] and eat bread")?

Developing empathy for the unchurched elevates invitational ministry to a set of skills that can be practiced. With members who have attended church their whole lives, this could be a challenge. They may have trouble imagining what it would be like not to be affiliated with a religious organization, but as they practice invitational ministry and talk more and more with people who have not grown up in church, empathy will come more naturally.

Another difference between evangelism and invitational ministry is that invitational ministry seeks to change the organization to produce a change in the individual, and seeks to change the individual to produce a change in the organization's culture. It is cyclical: when people change, they create a different culture within the organization, and a different culture changes the lives of individuals. Changing the organization doesn't make any sense if that organization is not, in turn, changing its members. An organization can only do what the individuals design it to do.

Barriers to Overcome

The practice of invitational ministry seeks to transform the members of the congregation to be disciples who transform the organizational culture. The strategy is to equip the congregation to move out of their comfort zone, snuggly secure within their sanctuary, to the discomfort of an unfamiliar place—both emotionally, as practicing a new ministry may cause some anxiety, and physically, as they practice that ministry outside of the church. Initially, some will express feeling incompetent or inadequate to practice invitation: "I won't be able to do this," and, "I don't know what to say." Leaders will help members manage the anxiety rather than move too quickly to suppress it and lose the opportunity to help members change their lives.

Some congregations have developed defeatist attitudes that enable the avoidance of anxiety. They assume something won't work before they even try it. If the practice does not provide a guarantee that it will work the first time, they struggle to find the momentum to get it off the ground. If they have attempted to attract people to worship or a program and did not perceive that these efforts were successful (however success was defined), then they are unlikely to want to try something else. This mind-set can hold a congregation hostage. They stop trying anything. Fear of failure immobilizes them. In time, they are confronted by the decline in members and money.

Changing the culture of congregational life is not easy. We begin by assessing if the congregation is experiencing comfort, discomfort (anxiety), or such severe discomfort that it is depressed. I find that congregations that are comfortable have little incentive to want to do things differently. Depressed congregations cannot access the energy to do things differently. In these two conditions of congregational life, change is unlikely for both the individual or the organization. When the depressed congregation does make a change, it is often a quick fix to alleviate whatever is causing the anxiety at the moment. When the problem returns, it usually makes them even more discouraged and depressed.

Congregations most receptive to practicing invitational ministry are the ones who are willing to change the organization to make changes in the lives of individuals. If worship is not meeting the spiritual needs of the churched and the unchurched, then the congregation may need to change the way in which it worships. Their mission is not to survive and remain open, but to continually assess how effective the organization is at forming the faith of individuals so that they may thrive. Congregational life is described as "a learning environment" in which disciples can acquire new skills. To create momentum, the congregation's members need to become aware of their discomfort and have hope that, by making these changes, they will move to a better place.

Building Relationships through Events

Whereas evangelism seeks to bring people to worship as the first point of contact with a religious organization, invitational ministry invites them to an event, such as a movie or a concert or a luau. Invitational ministry does not expect that the unchurched should want to "do" church the way that it has always been done.

By building relationships with the unchurched at events, the churched can find out about their neighbors' spiritual needs. Too often, instead of investing the time in relationships and conversations, the churched simply try to guess what the unchurched are looking for in a religious organization (and often they guess incorrectly). Invitational events offer an opportunity for the churched to forge relationships and have these conversations. They can ask open-ended questions about musical preferences, for example, or, if the people seem interested in spiritual matters, what kind of a situation is most conducive to talking about faith.

Invitational Ministry Prioritizes the Spiritual Needs of Those Not in Church

Because invitational ministry prioritizes the spiritual needs of the unchurched so as to make disciples of them, members must be willing to sacrifice a percentage of their own spiritual needs. If the worship service is designed to meet the needs of the churched 100 percent of the time, the unchurched are the ones who sacrifice what they need. As the past has shown, though, they are not inclined to do this, and, therefore, will not return to worship. So a congregation has to think, pray about, and discuss giving up the emphasis on their own spiritual needs (unless they want the congregation to continue to decline) and working toward meeting the spiritual needs of the unchurched so that they can become disciples of Jesus. Fortunately, as members become invitational ministers they find that the practice itself makes up for what they give up, tenfold.

Let me share an example from my own experience. The minister of music came to me one day and told me that he had put together a punk-alternative praise band, comprised of young people in the congregation who played an instrument. He asked if they could play during the worship service. Honestly, I don't like that kind of music, and I knew there would be members of the congregation who didn't like that kind of music either. My mind immediately went to Monday morning and the parade of upset members knocking on my door. So my first response to the music minister was, "No way." Later on, I prayed about it, though. God reminded me that the congregation had covenanted to become multicultural, which meant that worship was not about meeting any one person's spiritual needs all the time. So I gave my full support to the idea.

On the Sunday morning when they were schedule to play, I was anxious. My stubborn heart had a twinge of regret, still fearing that some members would say we had gone too far. And then I looked up in the balcony and saw about fifty young people having a good time in worship, rocking back and forth and singing along. I remember confessing, "It's not about me." I would rather have young people in worship than expect the worship leader to meet my spiritual needs alone. Singing one less traditional hymn in order to learn a new one, inviting people to witness to their faith during the service, or being willing to experiment with new ways of praying and meditating raises the potential to meet the spiritual needs of everyone. It taps into new places within the spiritual life of those who go to church as well as those coming to worship for the first time. Diversity of worshipers has a different energy than when everyone is of the same cultural grouping. Church members can testify that worshiping with people new to church has helped them to benefit spiritually in ways they never imagined possible.

Chapter 2

Why Practice
Invitational Ministry?

It matters why we practice invitational ministry. As members begin inviting their friends and family, neighbors and strangers to invitational events, these people will ask why they are being invited. In communities where the church has been disconnected from its neighbors for some time, those neighbors will also ask, "Why now?" Misguided members may respond, "Our church has had to use its endowment to pay our pastor the last few years, and so we've decided that a better option is to reach out for new members with the hope of bringing in more money." But frankly, our friends, family members, and neighbors do not want to help us save our beloved organization. These are the interests of the churched, not the unchurched. People do not want to be invited for their money; in fact, they are already apprehensive that the only reason a member would invite them is "because the church wants my money." Membership drives and fund-raising activities are not avenues for practicing invitational ministry.

This chapter examines the motivational factors for numerical church growth and tries to align those factors with the call to practice invitational ministry. Initially, these reasons may be quite different. A congregation often wants to grow numerically because they expect, or at least hope for, an increase in tithes and offerings. The motivation of money should not be considered a faithful reason to reach out, and the persons invited will probably say no if they suspect this is why they are being asked. Members who invite their friends for the purpose of increasing the annual budget risk losing those friendships. If we try to hide it from them or give them another reason that covers up the real reason, they may come and suspect they have been lied to and feel betrayed. "Is that why you invited me to the event?" Remember, newcomers do not want to come to church to meet the needs of the church. They will only be willing to come when the church provides them with something that sparks their interest and/or meets their needs.

Nevertheless, most congregations begin thinking about numerical church growth because of organizational factors. The problem is usually identified as "not enough money" and the immediate solution is "more members." Lack of money appears to be the problem because several members have done the math and, if the current financial trend continues, the church will be forced to close. This possibility causes anxiety and can lead a congregation to function in panic mode. "We have to do something now!" Focusing on getting more members is the tactic of choice to alleviate the anxiety. Church members may even talk about how great it would be to have plenty of money by filling the sanctuary with new people on Sunday morning, just like in the glory days. Everyone is in agreement that this solution is the most attractive, and should be pursued—until someone asks, "And how are we going to accomplish this?"

Some congregations will identify the problem as "not enough members" because, though they continue to remain financially solvent (thanks in part to a generation who gave their life savings to carry on the excitement of what was happening in the church during the 1960s), there are not enough members to complete all the tasks obliged by the structure and by-laws of the organization.[1] Members express feeling worn-out from "wearing so many hats," and complain that the new people are not getting involved and doing their fair share. (New people do not have the same interest in coming to church to do organizational tasks.) The nominating committee becomes increasingly frustrated because members run the other way when approached to serve on a committee. People are asked to do something, not because they have a passion for it, but because the functioning of the organization demands the task is done. The organization begins to seem like an insatiable plant begging constantly to be fed, just like in *The Little Shop of Horrors*.[2]

To begin moving away from the mind-sets I've described, pastors and church leaders may ask members to think about why they want to practice invitational ministry. The intention of this exercise is to help them identify problems further below the surface, beyond "money" and/or "members." By naming the symptoms, they can venture to find out why the congregation is in decline. Congregations generally are not gaining new members because they are not meeting the spiritual needs and interests of people outside the church. During this exercise, members may come to a place where they are able to be more transparent. "Yes, lack of money was the initial reason why we began to pray about reaching out, but God revealed to us that there were so many other reasons. These reasons helped us to better identify how we could change ourselves in order to be disciples for Jesus." *Money is not a good reason to reach out* to the unchurched. Hopefully, through prayer, members can begin to identify better reasons that benefit the lives of individuals, such as personal transformation. Members want to do ministry, not manipulate their friends and family to do something they don't want to do.

Discerning What God Wants for the Congregation

The congregation must first decide if moving forward is what God wants for them. If money and members are in decline, it is a good time to assess whether God wants them to survive. When a congregation makes an appointment with me for consultation, I ask them to pray for several weeks to determine whether or not they believe that God wants them to thrive. (Notice that I use the word "thrive," not "survive." What fun is it to get stuck in survival mode?) It doesn't make much sense to try to grow a congregation numerically if God is signaling otherwise.

Too often, the issue of money and the membership produces so much anxiety and expends so much energy that a congregation has been negligent in its practice of prayer. They are well aware of what they want, but less sure of what God wants for them. Instead of making statements such as, "This is what I want for the future of my church," the congregation needs to reach a consensus about what they believe that God wants for the direction of Jesus' church. The way to reach this consensus is to pray individually, and then to gather together collectively for prayer and conversation.

(As an aside, this also moves members toward feeling more comfortable talking about their faith.)

It's true that a church's lack of money can motivate members to reach out to their community in new ways. We could start by chastising them for this drive, but instead I recommend that leaders affirm this as an opportunity for a new spiritual journey. An incentive is still an incentive. Leaders can use this momentum to move forward. While we want to start where people are on that journey, we should and can move them to another place. Leaders and members should pray together about what kinds of outreach efforts might get them to feel excited, and which ones promise new ways of reconnecting with their community

The success of creating a culture of invitation depends on getting everyone on board. The more people involved from the beginning, the more likely a congregation is to change its culture to be more aligned with its new missional focus. If the decision is made by a few serving on a committee or by those who have historically held power in the church, there will be others who remain entrenched in their own self-serving interests. If they are not included in the collective prayer and conversation, they will be less likely to support and participate in creating this new culture. The decision reached after praying about all the alternatives needs to be made by consensus, not by voting, after everyone has prayed and everyone (or at least almost everyone—some people will remain holdouts for a variety of reasons) believes that this is what God wants for the future. If a number of people are apathetic or feel left out of the process, it will be difficult for those trying to implement change to navigate around and through their resistance.

As the congregation prays and considers alternatives, the members may also keep in mind that the only unfaithful decision is to avoid making any decision at all. Continuing to do things the same way and expecting that things will be different down the road is a sign of denial. Congregations that close without ever making a decision often reflect back and realize how embedded they were in denial. They hoped that the problems would go away. With a worship bulletin in hand, they waited patiently by the front door for all the new people to arrive. They were afraid that if they closed the church that meant that they had "failed" each other and God. These congregations recount that the fear of failure kept them immobilized. Eventually, the reality of their lack of finances became so painfully obvious that the decision was made for them. They had no other choice but to close their doors. Congregations that have walked this path testify that they wished they had been more willing to embrace change before they reached the point when they had no options left.

Practicing prayer and trying to be faithful to what God wants is an exercise in spiritual formation. Prayer is the best way to move a congregation away from a deer-in-the-headlights gaze and the "money and members" mantra. Arriving at a shared belief that "this is what God wants" will help a congregation to meet challenges, overcome obstacles, and walk with faith and hope through moments of anxiety, fear, and frustration. Shifting away from the symptoms of congregational depression toward spiritual formation creates a new vision and the momentum for starting something innovative. Energy is redirected from constantly putting out fires and placing Band-Aids on that which hurts and is bleeding, to imagining all the possibilities for new ways to spiritually form faith.

Alternatives to Practicing Invitational Ministry

Leaving a Legacy by Helping Other Churches

Some congregations will run out of members before they run out of money. Depending on denominational policies and other factors, the assets can assist other congregations with more potential for vitality and numerical growth. Churches in this situation will examine their finances and reach the conclusion that God would not want them to use that money to heat a large building for a few people to come to worship on Sunday morning, especially if that building is located in a neighborhood struggling to make sure that everyone has enough food.

These congregations look at their finances and decide that they are better invested in a congregation that is thriving. This faithful alternative approaches the decision as a matter of good stewardship: How can this money best be used for the mission of Jesus Christ? If the worship service is not bringing lost people to Jesus, but only maintaining those who were found years ago, is there another congregation that is more effectively reaching those who need to be found? Congregations that choose this alternative often come to the conclusion, "We are no longer fulfilling our mission in this neighborhood, but we see that the congregation in the city is doing a great job, so we want to support them by giving them our money." Some members may even choose to attend that congregation after they close their church. When they see all the young people sitting in the pews, and they know that the legacy money is going to support thriving ministries, the giving congregation will realize that they made a faithful decision.

The "Plan a Date to Close" Alternative

Not every congregation will have the money to leave a legacy for another congregation. Instead, they have themselves to offer to another congregation. They have examined their finances and realize that they do not have enough money to continue to pay their staff, be faithful to their mission projects, and pay their utility bills. They may feel that are not able to choose this alternative, because of lack of money and members, but they can choose how they will handle this situation. I suggest that they hire a certified public accountant (and not a church growth consultant) to go over their assets and map out a plan based on how long they can continue to practice sound stewardship and worship in their building with their current pastor. This assessment helps them to select a date to close. From then on, they can relax and have fun. No longer anxious about what will become of their church, they can celebrate the years of ministry that the congregation did within its community. This approach puts a positive spin on their closing: the church served the needs of the community for many years but has outlived that purpose. It's time to let go.

Called to a Turnaround

After praying, some congregations will believe that God wants them to continue but to repurpose themselves to meet the interests and needs of another generation, an alternative sometimes called a "turnaround." Too often, however, congregations decide they want to do a turnaround without doing their homework. This is wishful thinking—imagining that just by making this choice, a turnaround will happen. They miss the memo that tells them, "*You* have to make this happen." They may be wishing that a church growth consultant will meet with them and bring her magic wand. Turning around the decline of the last fifty years, I tell them, is the most challenging mission that the congregation will undertake.

Congregations that successfully turn around the numerical decline and begin to grow again are cognizant of the difficulty that lies ahead. They brace themselves for the changes that will be coming, knowing these changes will not be geared toward meeting their own spiritual needs. They don't say, "Let's wait until they come before we make any major changes." They say, "If we don't make the changes now, they will never come." They feel passionate that God wants their church to continue to meet the spiritual needs of another generation, so they adopt a "whatever it takes" attitude. Instead of letting the decline continue, they take control of the situation with the help of the Holy Spirit and attempt something new—something outside of their comfort zone. They ask God to help them to manage their anxiety. They believe with all their hearts that Jesus needs them to do his work.

Spiritual Benefits of Numerical Church Growth

If the congregation believes it is called to a turnaround, keeping the benefits of practicing invitational ministry in the forefront of people's minds also helps them to tolerate the changes that will be needed to reverse the decline. Many good things will happen along the way, surprising graces that affirm the congregation is being faithful to the mission of Jesus. The organization benefits because, as numerical church growth takes place, the congregation accesses its spiritual energy to discover and implement new practices for the spiritual formation of the individual. Individuals also benefit because they are learning new skills for ministry and feeling more confident. This practice strengthens their faith, helping them learn new things about themselves and their relationship with God. Members sense that their participation in the life of this congregation makes a difference in the lives of others.

Another benefit of numerical church growth is that adding members usually increases a congregation's ability to expand its resources, such as offering more intergenerational programs. The smaller a congregation becomes, the more likely that the only opportunity for spiritual formation is a weekly worship service.

Programs such as marriage enrichment, Bible study, and bringing in experts on subjects such as parenting convey a message to the community that the church cares about them and is attempting to address some of their concerns. I am not advocating for a "bigger is better" approach to congregational vitality. However, the more resources a congregation can access, the more it can work toward meeting the spiritual needs of the current members—as well as those they hope to reach in the community.

The more resources available to a congregation, the more likely they also offer opportunities for other ministries, such as education, caring, and social justice. For those who do not yet think they have the skills for certain projects, whether visiting an elderly person or building a house, the more people, the more likely that someone can teach these skills. Programs that equip people with the skills to visit, pray with others, provide hospitality, or speak publicly provide people with ways to raise their own self-esteem. A congregation in decline usually defines its ministries based on organizational needs, whereas a numerically growing congregation often connects people with opportunities to live out their passion.

It also follows that the numerically larger a congregation becomes, the more likely it will reflect the demographics of American society, with respect for age, sexual orientation, race, ethnicity, ability, and socioeconomic status. A good reason to grow a congregation, especially when the church is located in an ethnically diverse neighborhood (of a five-to-ten-mile radius, depending on geography), is because this increases the likelihood of diversity. Small congregations can take stances and argue about whether or not they all agree in matters of sexuality. Larger congregations will not be able to convince everyone to be on the same page about any issue (and that is not a congregation's purpose) and so, instead, will work toward helping diverse people learn to interact with one another and deal with difference.

Learning the skills for invitational ministry and being able to successfully go out into the neighborhood and invite friends and family to church increases a congregation's capacity for trying new things. Once members feel they have succeeded with these efforts (measurable as numerical church growth), they may be more willing to try other ministries. They are less afraid of failure and begin to believe that when they take on a project, it is likely to produce the desired result. They no longer hoard resources for a rainy day because they see that when they use energy, that energy returns to them tenfold. New ideas aren't stomped upon for fear that someone's arm will be twisted to try to implement them. Rather, new ideas for ministries are prayed about and explored as a gift of new possibilities given by the Holy Spirit. People become excited again about the future of their church.

New skills, new opportunities for ministry, and new excitement in the church work together for spiritual formation. Individuals begin to feel better about their identity as disciples, more confident and assured that their ministry will make a difference in someone else's life. They may look for new ways of being involved in congregational life that they might not have been as willing to try before. This new outlook may extend to other areas of their lives as well. They may also be willing to take on new tasks at work or learn new skills to improve their job performance. As they learn to relate to others by practicing empathy and active listening, they bring these skills to their relationships with family and friends outside of the church. Practicing different behaviors makes us feel differently about ourselves. Behaviors that we perceive as successful (in that they accomplish what we expect them to accomplish) increase self-esteem, which leads to healthier living.

The secondary gain of numerical church growth is the overall improved functioning of the organization, which only exists as long as it meets the needs and interests of individuals. Organizations do have a kind of "collective soul" that experiences emotions and affects the emotional life of individuals. Like individuals, organizations can suffer from shame and low self-esteem. When members learn new skills and believe that they are doing the work that Jesus calls them to do, they feel better about themselves and their relationship with the organization; that good feeling translates into a collective good feeling. This is one of the most effective ways to heal congregational depression. On a vitality-depression continuum, the more the disciples are able to develop new skills and use their gifts for ministry, the closer the organization's soul moves toward experiencing vitality.

Chapter 3

The Mission Field

When discussing invitational ministry with members of a congregation, inevitably someone will lament, "But everyone I know is already churched!" My friend Darrell Cruz, a pastor in Reading, Pennsylvania, says, "If you are a disciple of Jesus and all your friends are churched, then you need a new set of friends!" Invitational ministry equips disciples to make new friends in the immediate neighborhood by holding invitational events. A team in the congregation will gather to plan these events. To assist them in their planning, invitational ministers need to identify what is known as "the mission field." Generally speaking, these are the people who live in a three-mile radius around the church building (although this can be narrowed or widened depending on geography and population density). The closer people live to the church, the more likely they are to attend.

This chapter seeks to answer questions relating to the mission field. The first set of questions explores how a congregation becomes disconnected from its neighbors and how to create interest among the current members to reach out and reconnect. The second set of questions examines the neighborhood and its lifecycle in order to determine the best way to reach out. The third set of questions focuses on who is currently living in the neighborhood, so that we can make certain assumptions about their needs and interests.

How Does a Church Disconnect from Its Community?

Beginning in the 1950s, suburban churches experienced an influx of families moving into their mission fields from the city and urban areas. As these young families purchased homes, they sought out the local churches of their parents' denomination. For about twenty years, most suburban congregations significantly increased in membership; for many, this was the time when there were so many children in the Christian education program that educational wings were built onto the church buildings. To accommodate the needs and interests of these new young families, many congregations added to their ministry staff, calling an associate pastor, a youth minister, and/or a Christian education director. Congregations flourished.

Two factors came into play. One, congregations offered social events for these new young families to help them develop friendships. These are the same friendships today that the current (aging) membership still maintain. People moved into the neighborhood and were invited to meet new friends by attending a social event at the church. In time, the flight to the suburbs slowed down and those who were now friends within the congregation shifted these events to serve the needs of members. Potluck dinners, game nights, and women's fellowship groups focused on the current membership.

The redirected focus on the current membership produced what members often express as "a family feeling." This close-knit sense of stability complemented the reality of "staying put" in their neighborhood; families who purchased homes in the 1950s often stayed in those homes most of their lives, until perhaps they needed nursing care.

The economic ability to purchase a home instead of renting created conditions in which people were more likely to invest in friendships, knowing that others would also be around for the long term. Back then, the church became the center of people's social lives. Members felt close to other members, but at the same time they are disconnected from new people moving into the neighborhood. With the old members dying and new people not consistently coming to church, numerical decline was inevitable.

The second factor that contributes to a congregation becoming disconnected from its neighborhood is when those moving into the neighborhood represent a different ethnic grouping than those who have been living there. In neighborhoods that offer affordable housing, there is often a culture of transition that allows for an ethnic group to move in, get acclimated, raise their socioeconomic status, and then move out. Then the next group moves in, and so forth. What is happening in some congregations is that they perceive they are unable to attract those from a particular ethnic group who are different from the current membership. Based on the diverse demographic, they give up on being invitational ministers and submit to the decline.

When neighborhoods transition from one ethnic group to another, those in the first ethnic group who can afford to move out often do so. In my home church, Salem United Church of Christ in Harrisburg, Pennsylvania, almost all the members commute in across the Susquehanna River from the west shore. At one time, they all lived in the neighborhood, but Harrisburg has gone through a transition that brought an influx of different ethnicities. I joined the church because it is becoming ethnically diverse. But our mission field is not from the west shore, where there are plenty of other churches. Few people from the west shore will have any interest in crossing a very long bridge (legend says that Susquehanna is an Indian word meaning "mile wide, foot deep") into a very different cultural environment without having had a prior connection there. So we are focusing on bringing into our membership those in the immediate neighborhood of the church, because the people living close by are the future of our congregation.

How Do We Create Interest in Reconnecting with the Neighborhood?

Only a generation ago, those who were raised attending church became parents who often chose not to raise their own children to attend church. Older members express frustration that their adult children are not bringing their grandchildren to church: "I raised her to go to church. I don't understand why she isn't bringing my grandchildren to church." They say they have asked their adult children countless times to come to worship. Every time they ask, their adult children shrug their shoulders and respond that they are too busy with other activities. Their adult children may feel guilty because they know they have disappointed their parents. What tends to happen as a result is that members stop asking in favor of preserving their relationship. "I can't continue to argue with my son about bringing his children to church." Few of us could have anticipated that our own grandchildren would one day be among the unchurched!

While members may *say* they don't know anyone who doesn't go to church, they often do. They know that their adult children do not attend, but they feel some shame about this. One member may not be aware that another member feels this way because they have not had the opportunity to have this conversation. Doing so often frees members to talk about something that concerns them (and is one more example of moving away from being friends toward being sisters and brothers in Christ and having more intimate conversations).

Beginning with the mission field of adult children of current members is sometimes a good place to start reaching out. Adult children who grew up attending this particular church and have a relationship with the building that invokes a warm feeling may be likely to want to attend again. If they simply got out of the swing of attending church while in college and now have children of their own, they may be easy to engage to reenter the congregation. But this involves one important caveat: *as long as they live in the immediate neighborhood.* People who do not live in the neighborhood will come for a while, especially adult children who feel pressure to honor their parent's wishes, but, in time, they will feel less obligated. Their children may not know other children in the Sunday school because they live in a different neighborhood. A church filled with people who are commuting in, for whatever reasons, is a congregation that is headed toward the challenge of decline.

One reason to start with family members who live close to the church is that members tend to feel passionate about an outreach mission that focuses on people they care the most about: their children and grandchildren. They are more willing to learn and practice invitational skills if they stand to personally benefit. Furthermore, members are more willing to tolerate changes to the worship service—such as more contemporary music—if it raises the probability that their own children will attend. They tend to be less anxious about inviting their children and are eager to test out new ways of framing an invitation that might be more effective. They attend the workshops on how to do this because they are envisioning their children and grandchildren in the pews.

Members are also more likely to invite people whom they know than people they do not yet know. The former are in their daily lives; they already have relationships and it may follow that they are more likely to respond positively. It may be that the unchurched who have relationships with one who is churched trust that the churched person has their best interests at heart when an invitation is offered. The incentive for the churched person is not money or membership, but because he or she cares about those unchurched friends or acquaintances. This presents a different dynamic than developing new relationships with the unchurched.

The benefits of inviting the adult children of the current membership are twofold: (1) New people start coming and spiritual energy tends to increase. People feel good about these outreach efforts, even if partly self-serving. With some young families in the pews, other young families who are visiting are more likely to return a second Sunday. (2) The perceived success of attracting their children and grandchildren can motivate them to reach out to other people's adult children (not necessarily of the same denomination). Now, given that they were able to use their invitational skills to attract people they already have a relationship with, such as family members and friends, they may feel more at ease engaging people who live in the community whom they do not yet know.

The risk to starting here, with the adult children of the current members, is that the inviting can also end here. Mission accomplished. Those members whose adult children don't live in the neighborhood may express hope that another congregation will be willing to reach out to their adult children. Denominations need to keep track of the movement of a generation who is on the move, and could create a database of their adherents moving into new neighborhoods. However, the church cannot and should not depend exclusively on family members and friends of the churched, for there are plenty of unchurched people who have spiritual needs that can be met by the church.

Is the Neighborhood "Up and Coming" or "Been There and Declining"?

Neighborhoods have life cycles during which they are revitalized and considered "up and coming," seem to peak in real estate value, and then, with time, move into a phase of "been there and declining." Discerning what point in this cycle describes the neighborhood can be helpful to a congregation getting to know the mission field–for several reasons. First, and perhaps foremost, if people are moving into the neighborhood, they may be looking for opportunities to get to know others, similar to the movement of the 1950s and 1960s. Second, the economics of a neighborhood provide valuable information as to what may be the community's social service needs. A congregation that wants to reach out to the neighborhood and convey that it cares has to know what to care about. And third, many congregations are unaware of the shift in demographics, especially those members who have moved away, and therefore they don't know who is currently living in their neighborhoods.

An "up and coming" neighborhood is one that people are desiring to move into, because that neighborhood has become more affordable, or is designed for convenience or some other more trendy factor. Perhaps new businesses are popping up in local storefronts. Shops, restaurants, health clubs, and cafes are making their way into becoming a staple of the neighborhood's culture. A "been there and declining" neighborhood is on the other side of its life cycle. Real estate value is decreasing, businesses are closing, and the conversation in the neighborhood reflects people's desire to move out.

Neighborhoods in the process of being revitalized represent a window of opportunity for declining congregations to reinvent themselves. Just as the church of 1960 reached out to people moving out of the cities into the suburbs, the urban revitalization movement presents a unique opportunity for many congregations. Whoever is able to purchase those new homes is the mission field.

An up and coming neighborhood usually is investing in the school system, cleaning up parks and putting in more contemporary looking swing sets and jungle gyms, and taking care to beautify recreational areas for sports and family outings. The downtown area is being revitalized as new stores and coffee shops are appearing. Seating for people outside a restaurant in a city setting, with bar stools and a lively atmosphere, suggests that this neighborhood is a happening place. Young people may not be able to afford to move into a neighborhood that is up and coming, but they are particularly interested in these urban settings. Churches in urban areas that are up and coming should be aware that this is their opportunity to attract those who are moving in, both the young and not-so-young.

Been there and declining neighborhoods paint a different picture. The conversation may be about how they are experiencing more crime than in the past, and people are concerned for their safety because of violence and drugs. Stores are closing and relocating to areas that are up and coming. One may notice "for lease or sale" signs on storefronts, suggesting that they are unable to economically sustain themselves because their customer base cannot afford their services and/or is moving out of the neighborhood. Churches located in been there and declining neighborhoods have certain challenges to overcome. In some areas, they may need to expand their mission field beyond their immediate neighborhood to increase the number of unchurched they can reach, or offer something unique and different that will give people reason to commute in.

Assessing a Neighborhood

Congregations may need assistance to determine whether they are in an up-and-coming neighborhood or a declining one. A real estate broker, school officials, or local businesspeople will likely be able to provide answers to such questions as:

• Are young people moving into this neighborhood?
• Are there a number of coffee shops and cafes to walk to?
• Are investors investing in this neighborhood with shops, bars, and restaurants?

Drive around the neighborhood, looking for empty storefronts for lease. As real estate declines, some neighborhoods that attempt to revitalize will attract people to move in. Other neighborhoods that are declining may still attract those who have a memory of its past.

Too many congregations do not reach out because they think that their neighborhood is declining, when, in fact, the neighborhood is up and coming. Members tend to report, "Our neighborhood is declining because so many of our friends are moving out of the neighborhood." They do not seem to notice that another group of people has been buying their friends' homes and so replenishing the population. Members may fail to see the early signs of revitalization, and so also fail to join the process. A congregation that does not pay attention to these shifts often misses an opportunity to create a culture in the neighborhood in which the religious organizations figure prominently because they work toward helping the neighborhood through times of transition.

Who Is Currently Living in the Neighborhood?

Who is living in the neighborhood, and what are the demographics? Are young people able to afford the new homes being built? Too many congregations automatically say, "We want to attract young people," whether or not their neighborhood has many young people Can we make certain assumptions about our neighbors' needs and interests? Later, nearer the end of this chapter, I will suggest ways that invitational ministers can research these questions both by walking around the neighborhood and by doing searches on the Internet.

When members become aware of the groups of people now living in the church's neighborhood, they may not reach out because of certain preconceived expectations. For instance, when a neighborhood shifts to become predominately Latino, some Anglo congregations will concede to the often-cited statistic that Latinos tend to be either Catholic or Pentecostal. Demographic research does generally support the perception that the majority of Latinos may be already affiliated, but this does not mean that *every* Latino person and family living in the church's neighborhood is uninterested in mainline Protestantism.

Too often, a congregation uses a change in demographics to justify why it doesn't practice invitational ministry. Jesus doesn't call us to hang around with other disciples; he commissions us "to make disciples of all nations." The verse emphasizes *everyone,* as the Greek word *ethnos* forms the root of our English word *ethnicities.* Quite succinctly, Jesus tells his disciples to go out into their community to make disciples of people from all different backgrounds.

When a neighborhood changes demographics, it is an opportunity for a congregation to become multicultural. Churches that embrace the potential to become multicultural are more likely to survive during this time of decline. Young people are more interested in multicultural congregations, and many of them understand that worshiping in a multicultural congregation strengthens their own spiritual formation.[1]

It is far more faithful to invite everyone in the neighborhood and let them accept or decline, than not to invite people based on the assumption that they are connected with a church already. Members will need to adjust to hearing several "no's" before they hear one "yes" and change someone's life. If there is one Latino family who just moved into the neighborhood and is hoping for an invitation to the local mainline church, then members need to continue to ask Latino families until they find that one family. Along the way, members may find that several new families within the neighborhood have been hoping for an invitation.

Those who God has placed in the church's neighborhood are God's gift to the future of that church. We do not get to choose the mission field. It is chosen for us. Churches that are thriving are those whose members are inviting those who live in the immediate neighborhood.

As a working guideline, at least 80 percent of a congregation's membership should be drawn from a five-mile radius. Those who choose to commute from farther away are not the mission field, nor are their neighbors or friends. Thus, the church's mission field is about a five-mile radius (depending on the geography—e.g., rural).

What Are the Interests and Needs of the Mission Field?

We've established that the mission field—the area in which to focus most of your efforts—is the immediate neighborhood; roughly a five-mile radius around the church, taking into account other geographical features, such as mountains, waterways, and interstates. In well-populated areas with a number of other churches in close proximity, the circumference may be smaller. In more rural areas, a congregation may need to expand beyond five miles until it reaches a neighborhood with a number of unchurched people. The question is, How far are the unchurched willing to travel? The further away they live, the more interest a congregation needs to create in order to motivate them to drive that distance.

In times of economic hardship, many people are working multiple jobs and don't have free time for other activities. They are attracted to organizations that offer convenience. Geographic convenience influences people as they select a gym for working out, a coffee shop for meeting friends, and a grocery store to buy food. Convenience is also a significant factor in one's choice of religious organization. In fact, today this factor outweighs denominational loyalty. Location, access from the highway, visibility, ease of parking, and worship service times are all factors that contribute to the decision to attend a particular church.

This culture of convenience can be seen especially in areas undergoing urban revitalization. Young people are purchasing condominiums in areas where they can walk to restaurants, bars, and cafes. The inconvenience of having to get one's car out of the garage and drive to a suburban church is unappealing. A church in an urban area, then, has an advantage when it comes to attracting young people into its membership. They can walk to church. The church could market itself as "the church where everyone walks to attend worship." Walking to church can be considered a religious practice (as it is in Judaic orthodoxy). When other unchurched people see others walking into the building, they may become curious.

Increasingly, urban areas also provide bike paths along the main roads. An urban church should install bike racks as a sign of welcome. Members may prayerfully consider a bicycle ministry in which a group of cyclists gather at the church to bike to a sacred spot for meditative worship. A running club may also run to a place of nature, met there by the pastor (unless the pastor also could use some exercise!), who will say a prayer for them. Those who exercise in the morning perceive that they can exercise going to and from the church.

Along with location and convenience, the unchurched are more likely to show interest in a church that offers something of interest and perhaps appears different from their perceptions of what churches offer. The young generation does not have a lot of free time and has an abundance of choices about how to spend that time, so any energy that they are going to expend beyond work and play has to seem worthwhile. They are not bored and looking for something to fill their time. In a culture of multitasking, they seek opportunities to be involved in projects that both meet their spiritual needs and make a difference in the lives of other people. They tend to see those two goals as one and the same.

The young generation is searching for ways to make a difference in their communities. They are concerned about social problems such as hunger and homelessness, but are sometimes unaware of how to get involved in creating change and addressing these problems. Most people, not just the young, respond more positively when someone invites them to participate in a social justice project. The more active a congregation is in its immediate neighborhood—especially if the church is located in an urban or inner-city area—the more people in the neighborhood will look toward the church to gather, equip, and empower them to get involved in helping their community. The closer that the unchurched live to the church building and the more the church is perceived as caring about its community, the more likely people will be to participate in making a difference.

How Do We Get to Know Our Neighbors?

Opening the doors and venturing outside of the walls of the sanctuary can be life-changing for a congregation. When members start getting to know those who are on the other side, they are often surprised to discover how many interests and similar concerns they share. Those in the neighborhood are often surprised that "religious people" aren't the way that they had previously imagined. Once the churched and the unchurched take the first steps toward getting to know each other and building relationships, those in the community begins to realize that the members care about them. This realization creates interest in the church. The unchurched wonder, "What goes on in the church that makes them care about our community?"

Going out and exploring the neighborhood and meeting those who live in it may be new ventures for members. They will need to spiritually prepare themselves by believing that Jesus is calling them to do this. Without a theological reason to try a new behavior, most members won't do it. They need to be prepared to talk with people they do not know and practice their invitational skills. They may need to confront their prejudices and preconceived images of who the unchurched are, and remind themselves that these people are also children of God. These internal preparations will help provide the energy they need to move outside of their comfort zone and into the community.

Prayer Walks in the Neighborhood

A fun and healthy way to get to know the church's neighbors is to take a prayer walk. In teams of two (for keeping one another company and, in some neighborhoods, for safety), members walk around the community. I recommend that at least four teams go out at about the same time of day. They should do this at different times during the week, and even at different times during the calendar year. Some communities sponsor seasonal events, such as fireworks and the lighting of the Christmas tree. These events allow you to see masses of people in one sighting and pray for all of them. During the winter months, neighbors tend to hibernate. In the summer months, you may discover lots of activity, depending on where you live. Prayer teams should blend in with what everyone else is doing. I recommend doing prayer walks by walking, not by bike or in cars, because walking provides more opportunities to interact with people while gathering information about the community.

Prayers can be voiced out loud or in silence, depending on the team's preference. In some neighborhoods, people may believe that you are there to pray over them because you think they are going to hell, and they may be offended by this idea. So when in question, it is better to pray silently. The idea is not to change those for whom you are praying, but to pray for the invitational ministers (the team) who are trying to discern what the needs of the community are and how they might help. The point of this exercise is to make visible to the congregation that which has been hidden. Prayer teams may come back with statements such as, "I wasn't aware that there were so many empty storefronts," or, "I didn't realize that so many Spanish- speaking people live in our neighborhood." When I am asked how long teams need to take these walks, I answer, "Until something surprises you."

Congregations usually have to let go of their preconceptions about who is in the neighborhood and instead make reliable observations. Seeing a playground may lead you to expect children, but an overgrown grass ball field may indicate that no one has played ball there for some time. Those expecting to see young families may be surprised to notice assisted living facilities.

With open minds and hearts, the team may discover the impact of the economic downturn and become aware of an increase in poverty. You might walk right past a home housing drug abuse or violence. Keep your eyes wide open to see the underlying problems. Every neighborhood has them. During these prayer walks, you must assume the presence of much that the naked eye cannot view; so pray that God will help you to see the physical, emotional, and spiritual needs of your neighbors. Then you may go about ministering to those needs through invitational ministry.

The following questions may be used to help you collect and interpret the needed information. After reading through the questions, your teams may discern which ones would be relevant to your neighborhood. You may want to add some questions of your own.

- What cultural groupings are you seeing—age, gender, race/ethnicity, abilities, and so on of those in your neighborhood?
- Do people seem happy, sad, depressed, hurried? How would you categorize the mood of your neighborhood?
- What are people doing? Are they walking, sitting, talking with other neighbors?
- Where do people gather? Do they go to local coffee shops, grocery stores, diners? If had you just moved into the neighborhood, where would you go to meet people? Is there a health club, gym, or spa? Do the meeting places offer wholesome activities, or more questionable, destructive activities like those associated with teen-age crime or gang activities?
- If you are walking in the evening, can you see television sets lighted through the windows? Does this suggest some isolation in your neighborhood, or are people just exhausted and in need of solitude and entertainment? What alternatives

would you expect to see? Some type of family activity or conversation or working on children's homework?

- Do people greet others whom they do not know? What is the culture toward the stranger? When you say "hi" to people, do they say "hi" back? How frequently does someone initiate the greeting? How readily do people interact with those whom they do not know?
- How much of a neighborhood "feel" is there? Is it a picture postcard scene, or is it more congested with buildings and cars?
- From your observations, why do you think that people choose to move into this neighborhood? Is it convenient access to the highway? Are the schools rated highly?
- Do you notice religious symbols in various places–people's front lawns, rear windows of cars, storefronts, street corners? Which religion is associated with these symbols?
- Are people walking pets?

Using the Internet for Data Collection

Data and statistics can give you some insight about who your neighbors are and about the culture of your neighborhood. Several Internet resources offer statistics on your neighborhood. Some denominational offices pay an annual fee for their congregations to be able to access services that compile extensive information and package this information into a usable form.[2] The Internet itself offers several helpful ways to collect data. Sites that are free can be accessed by typing "city data" into a search engine, along with the zip code or location of your church building. The following questions will get you started with doing neighborhood research via the Internet.

- Is this a more liberal or conservative (politically and religiously) neighborhood? Has that changed recently in light of political trends?
- Are children likely to be involved in sports? What day and time of the week do these sports play? When do they practice?
- What is the fastest growing ethnic group in your neighborhood? Which group is projected to be the fastest growing in the

next twenty-five years? Which ethnic group is likely to decline?

- On trulia.com, you can track the value of real estate. Has the church's neighborhood been increasing or decreasing in value over the past six months?
- What is the average income? What do people do for a living?
- Is there a developer or an investor considering putting in a new development? Who do they project will be interested in purchasing these homes?
- What are the social service needs of the community?

Chapter 4

Invitational Events

Recently I consulted with a congregation who felt called to reach out to invite the young people in their neighborhood to an invitational event. They decided that they would hold a free concert on the front lawn of their church, visible and easily accessible to everyone in the neighborhood. Members hung up signs in local coffee shops, stores, and health clubs. They practiced their newly acquired invitational skills and invited friends and family members. In the planning phase, they were excited and hopeful that this event would help them to get to know the neighbors. But when I met with them to evaluate the success of the event, they were disappointed. Many of their unchurched friends, neighbors, and family members had attended, but not the young people they hoped would come. Wondering about this, I inquired, "Who did you hire to play at the concert?" They responded, "A Lawrence Welk tribute band." Gently, I said, "I think I know what happened..."

The reason to identify the mission field is so that we can offer events that will interest them. Congregations either think they already know who is in the mission field and therefore bypass this step in the process (see chapter 3), or they think that what is of interest to them will be of interest to everyone, regardless of age or ethnic background. The success of invitational events depends on getting to know who is in the neighborhood before planning invitational events.

Church members may assume they know the interests of their family and friends, yet if they have invited family and friends to worship and been turned down, then they may not be as aware as they think. For instance, some aging congregations assume that the traditional music they sing meets the spiritual needs of every age range. Getting to know young people at an invitational event is a chance to learn whether this is true, or if they need to make changes to the music in worship in order to accommodate the different needs among young people.

The purpose of identifying the mission field and holding the first few invitational events is to get to know those not attending church and be better equipped to plan additional events (and eventually, worship) that will meet their spiritual needs and interests. People inside and outside of church have similar spiritual needs, but the way their faith is formed is likely to be quite different, given that some have formed their faith through practices within a religious organization and some have formed their faith outside organized religion. While both groups seek a spiritual experience of God that strengthens their relationship, each group encounters this experience from a different place. One of the major differences is that people in church form their faith in community, through relationships with other believers. People who do not attend church often form their faith in solo activities, though some secular groups (such as twelve-step groups) have a spiritual component. From a theological standpoint, invitational events give people an opportunity to experience God in community.

Invitational events also help people discern their interests and spiritual needs. In the process, some already in church may identify some needs that they have a yearning to fulfill. For example, people not affiliated with a church or with a particular religion may be interested in the similarities and differences between global religions. Even if they proclaim themselves to be Christian, they are interested in learning about different practices. Those who are involved in church may perceive that showing any interest in someone else's religious viewpoint may lure one away from one's own religion. But an event exposing them to other religions may actually help them appreciate the uniqueness of their own.

Spiritual needs come in all shapes and sizes, and may or may not be generalizable to age and/or gender. People within the same age group may not all like the same kind of music. Some may have needs for quiet time because their jobs entail daily interaction with others. Others may be looking for opportunities to learn new skills. It's difficult to identify one or two spiritual needs that apply across the board, especially given that each individual is really his or her own multicultural unit.

But age and ethnic background can be indicators of preference for such spiritual needs as music. Having a praise band in the worship service–once thought to be contemporary–now appears traditional among twenty-somethings. Their preference is often for Taizé or classical music. Those who are churched tend to be more in tune with their spiritual need for forgiveness (and thus are able to confess guilt), collective prayer, and community. The unchurched can teach the churched the value of alone time with God in daily life through practices such as yoga and meditation. Gathering together both the churched and the unchurched, identifying the diversity of spiritual needs, and discerning what a religious organization can offer to meet those needs holds much potential to spiritually benefit both groups.

What Are Invitational Events?

Most congregations spend time together laughing, crying, and everything in between. They do this to nurture and sustain their relationships with one another. When one member is experiencing a personal crisis, that member trusts that others will offer prayer and emotional support. Christians believe that God provides strength and comfort through the love and support of other believers in community. These relationships are instrumental to experiencing God's blessings. Members know the spiritual needs of one another because they have invested energy in getting to know each other. I deeply respect that most members have met their closest friends through church-held events, such as potluck dinners and movie nights, and that they cherish these relationships. But these activities are not invitational events.

Church activities are for people already in the congregation. The pastor announces that an event will be held on Friday night at the church and everyone should bring a covered dish. He or she will announce the event from the pulpit, as those who are in attendance are the ones who are expected to come. A few people may consider inviting someone in their neighborhood who could use a night out and likes covered-dish suppers, but inviting friends and family doesn't occur to most of the others. These activities I refer to as "all-church events." The purpose is to have fun with people with whom a relationship has already been developed. All-church events are a central aspect of congregational life and should be held on an ongoing basis to nurture these relationships.

An invitational event is different. A congregation feels called to reach out to the community and to invite friends, family, and neighbors to an event for the purpose of developing new relationships. By developing these relationships, church people can counteract misperceptions that everyone who attends a church is hypocritical and judgmental. And those who don't attend church can challenge the misperceptions that those who do not go to church do not believe in God.

Some congregations think having a presence at a community activity is an invitational event.

They pass out water bottles stamped with their church's name and picture, the premise being that the unchurched were not coming because they didn't know where the church was located and/or they weren't aware which denomination the church was affiliated with. In reality, they probably know where the church building is located, and they don't particularly care about the denomination. If the problem is that the unchurched have been trying to figure out where the church is located, then having a presence at a community event may be the solution. But in almost every situation of decline, informing the community about the name and location is not the problem to be solved.

Fund-raising is also not an invitational event. This is an important distinction because, for some congregations, the most popular events that draw the unchurched onto church property are fund-raising ones. Everyone loves a good yard sale, when "one person's trash becomes another person's treasure." A pancake breakfast may bring people in the neighborhood in droves for a good and inexpensive meal. Events that offer something of value will attract people for economic reasons. Fund-raising is also important to the life of a congregation, especially when the congregation is dependent upon the income to meet the budget. However, fund-raising and invitational events do not blend together. The purpose of fund-raising is to make money. Invitational events should help to dispel the myth that "the church only wants my money."

Large-Scale or Small-Scale Event, Low or High Interactive

Invitational events come in two sizes: small and large. For a small-scale event, the team plans an activity to which a few churched people will each personally invite an unchurched person to attend. An example would be a gathering at a member's house for dinner. Eight members of the church who like each other and have a close relationship may each invite one person to attend. Because they all like each other, they are likely to invite other people who will like each other. Small invitational events usually are between six and twenty people. The church may also plan a large-scale event that divides people into small groups (e.g., for dinner). The benefit of small groups is that the unchurched get to know a few people well and begin developing relationships. Examples include knitting groups (interest-based), small group faith-sharing, and helping out at a soup kitchen.

A large-scale event is one in which the planning team has little means of anticipating how many will attend. Each member who attends brings someone unchurched, and the congregation also sends out postcards to those in the neighborhood. Examples of large-scale events include concerts on the town green, family movie or game nights in the fellowship hall, a free swim at the local YMCA, or a night to have one's picture taken with a local celebrity. Large-scale events are usually something fun that will appeal to a large group of people.

Invitational events also come in two forms: low and high interactive. Basically, a low interactive event is one in which an unchurched person will meet a few other people, begin the process of building a relationship, and feel comfortable attending something that has to do, at least tangentially, with church. A high interactive event is one in which a group of churched and unchurched people gather for an intimate conversation about what is going on in their lives and how God is involved. Events are best planned on a continuum between low and high interactive, but the distinction is helpful. Few people want to begin their church involvement by being thrust into a small group of personal sharing.

They need time to develop relationships with each other. The purpose of low interactive events is to build relationships; the purpose of high interactive events is faith and personal sharing.

Small-scale invitational events tend to be high interactive ones, and large-scale invitational events are usually designed as low interactive. (An exception would be a small gathering at someone's house to watch the football game.) Examples of low interactive events are movies, concerts, watching a football game on television at a member's house, going to hear a speaker, etc. Low interactive events are activities in which one comes to watch and listen and be with other people. Slightly more interactive events include building a house for Habitat for Humanity with a group of people or holding a protest sign for a social justice cause. Alternatively, a high interactive event would be a sacred conversation on race, politics, or sexuality. High interactive events encourage the attendees to share their personal selves. A small group doing the exercises in the "Unbinding" series (see chapter 1) is a good example of a high interactive event.

Finding Energy for Invitational Events

Many congregations lament that they have made several attempts to reach out to their neighborhoods, yet their neighborhoods seemed disinterested. Members recall a series of events and programs that were offered, and the only people who attended were church members. If some did attend from the neighborhood, they did not return for worship the following Sunday morning. After a period of trying to get the unchurched to come to worship, and the unchurched not responding by attending, church members become frustrated and discouraged. A sense of feeling rejected may set in. A natural response to feeling rejected is to unconsciously reject those who make us feel this way first (so that we no longer feel rejected by them). This lingering feeling of rejection looms over the congregation as they watch the decline in their membership. They regress to the perception that the neighborhood is to blame for their internal woes. "If only the people in the neighborhood would come and support our church, we wouldn't be having these problems!" These emotions drive a congregation to become further disconnected from its neighborhood and focus inwardly. They begin to say things such as, "If they don't want to come to things we offer, then we should only offer activities that interest us. If they want to come, they know where to find us."

Deflated, dejected, and depressed, congregations with a history of trying to attract new members can be reluctant to try invitational events. Reluctance is often expressed as a lack of energy. "Who is going to plan and implement all these events? We have enough trouble trying to get people to serve on our governing board." The more a congregation perceives that its efforts do not lead to the desired results, the more it seeks to conserve energy, which appears to be in limited supply. Hopefully, members will come to realize that when they invest energy in a ministry that makes them feel more spiritually connected to God, their energy multiplies exponentially.

Congregations with low energy don't tend to invest that energy in discerning the needs and interests of the unchurched, and so they default to guessing what those interests might be. They offer invitational events that appeal to their own memberships and are designed to persuade people to come to worship, not to build relationships. They are willing to invest a *little* energy, but are hoping for *large* results (i.e., the pews being filled the following Sunday). Invitational events tend to work the other way around—a lot of energy invested to the get minimal results of a few new people attending. (But why underestimate the value of changing the life of just one person?) Realistic expectations need to be set so that the congregation will anticipate that their neighbors will need time to trust why the congregation is reaching out and respond with interest. A church that has appeared as a fortress for the past twenty years and now says, "We want you to come in," will need to offer enough events to do some convincing that their motivation is not for money and members, but to love thy neighbor.

Declining congregations tend to struggle with accessing energy. (Noting the decline itself can sap energy.) If the choice comes down to either holding an invitational event or continuing worship, then I advocate for holding an invitational event. If the worship service has not inspired people to practice invitation, then another forum may hold more potential for doing so. Members in declining congregations with low energy often reflect, "These are great ideas, but who is going to do all these things?" If they have prayed that a turnaround is what God wants, then they may need to reprioritize: if worship is not bringing people into the flock, then they need to try something else. Finding the energy to plan and implement invitational events is essential to the process. Skimping on investing energy and bypassing phases of the planning process are likely to undermine the congregation's efforts to grow numerically.

A Worship Sabbatical Can Free Up Energy

Planning worship takes much energy, as most pastors and worship leaders can attest. Pastors should focus their energy on equipping leaders to equip disciples for invitational ministry. The congregation should pray about taking a sabbatical from holding a formal worship service on Sunday morning. To do so frees up both the pastor's energy as well as the members'. By "formal," I refer to any activity that requires time to plan, such as sermon preparation, music rehearsals, writing the liturgy for the bulletin, etc. The energy expended for worship is usually in the preparation; the service itself should generate energy. The pastor may consider alternative forms of worship that generate energy but do not require a lot of energy for planning. For instance, holding a hymn sing and asking worshipers to light candles and say prayers, or asking the local high school if a drama club or music group would be willing to lead worship.

In this way, everyone's energy becomes focused on invitational events.

Taking a sabbatical from worship also gives declining congregations an opportunity to evaluate which forms of worship are effectively meeting their spiritual needs. For instance, members may talk openly about which aspects of the worship service they miss and which, they now realize, they could do without. The criterion for evaluating forms of worship is whether or not a form of worship—such as the sermon, call to confession, or anthem—inspires people to reach out to others. Such inspiration shows that the worship experience is moving faith to the next level. This exercise may help congregations try more creative ways to experience and communicate with God in conjunction with spiritual formation. A sabbatical from formal worship allows time to step back and look at your activity from a different perspective.

This balcony view may help you to discover and accept the reality that some forms of worship are not providing the spiritual energy you need to become invitational ministers. This discovery means these forms of worship are not meeting your spiritual needs.

During this sabbatical, the congregation also needs to engage in small group faith sharing in place of worship on Sunday morning. (This suggestion does not provide members a reason to start staying home on Sunday morning!) This small group faith sharing can be done in place of formal worship, or the worship can be extended to include this time. Invitational ministers will need to practice talking about their faith with other people. It is usually easier for them to practice with other members who themselves are trying to do learn how to do this. If visitors do appear at the door, they may or may not feel comfortable joining a group to talk about their faith. If they seem comfortable, the group may continue to share. If not, the group may be sensitive and ease into the conversation, being sure to make it easy and comfortable for the visitor to enter the conversation. The important thing to keep in mind is that *this is* an invitational event. Coming together to share faith is an example of a high interactive event.

Why Can't We Invite People Straight to Worship?

Relying on invitations to worship to connect people to church is the approach to numerical church growth that almost every mainline congregation has taken during the last twenty years. Signs out in front of the buildings read, "Everyone Is Welcome," and ushers are prepared to greet visitors by the doors. Some congregations have observed that there have been fewer visitors in recent years, marked by the decrease of interest in organized religion among the unchurched and the increasing number of those who identify themselves as spiritual but not religious. Most members are well aware that their friends and family members don't have interest in the current way they worship and that inviting them to worship is usually in vain. It has become evident that we need a different forum to interest the unchurched in religious organizations and meet their spiritual needs.

Most congregations think they are already meeting the spiritual needs of the unchurched in their worship services. To assess whether or not this is happening, I suggest the following exercise.

For several months, record how many visitors attend for the first time, and then how many of these people return a second Sunday. If the number of visitors who are not returning is higher than those who are, then it is likely that the worship service is not meeting their spiritual needs. If a congregation finds that it cannot do this exercise because it sees very few visitors, then the issue is one of whether the members of the church are practicing invitational ministry. Once they are practicing these skills and inviting the unchurched to worship after getting to know them at invitational events, if the unchurched are not returning a second Sunday, then the worship service is not meeting their spiritual needs–although the members *are* doing a good job of inviting them.

One reason to invite the unchurched to an event rather than worship has to do with the comfort factor among both the churched and the unchurched. Members are more likely to invite friends and family to an event, because to invite them to worship feels more personal. The churched seem to feel more comfortable inviting others to attend something that is more social in nature.

The unchurched also report feeling more comfortable attending an event rather than worship. Worship can be an intimidating experience for people who have never set foot in a sanctuary or have only occasionally attended a worship service. They don't know where to sit, why someone needs to show them where to sit, or what will happen next. The unchurched are often pleasantly surprised that someone says "hello" and welcomes them, because they assume that people don't know each other in a church (and therefore often don't understand the importance of community).

Someone who is unfamiliar with worship is unfamiliar with the norms, rituals, and expectations. Does one clap when one enjoys a musical selection? Perhaps the unchurched person thought the sermon was so inspiring that he or she whistles and shouts loudly when the pastors says, "Amen," in a culture where members remain silent. Members may not be so gracious for this error in etiquette and look disapprovingly in the visitor's direction. During communion, does one eat the bread first or wait until the communion cup is passed? Can one take seconds? Is it inappropriate to text during a worship service? When visitors arrive in jeans, they may feel uncomfortable if everyone else is dressed up in their Sunday best.

Some visitors observe that the other worshipers (that is, the members) don't look comfortable either (which may be a projection of the visitors' own discomfort). They notice that, during the sermon, some members are looking at their watches or cautiously glancing toward the clock in the back of the sanctuary. They interpret from these behaviors that people are bored. If they look around and a lot of people seem bored, then they are likely to conclude that worship is boring, *even if that is not their experience.* Members may tolerate boring worship out of a sense of obligation, but visitors do not feel obligated. They are making a choice about whether or not organized religion can help them to form their faith. Boring worship does not meet that need.

Interestingly, one congregation conducted a survey to ask visitors why they decided to return a second Sunday. The most common response was because they perceived that the worshipers believed what they were saying (creeds, responsive readings, etc.) and singing (hymns, *Gloria Patri,* doxology). A choir that sings an anthem with all that is within them, joyfully and enthusiastically, as if they are singing to Jesus standing before them, inspires interest among visitors. They reflect, "Wow, they really seem to believe!" The unchurched visitor may not necessarily believe in what is being said, but is intrigued when everyone else seems to believe. Somehow, being saturated in a community of believers (and cloud of witnesses) and by the strength of their believing is the most single influential variable in deciding to return to worship.

The unchurched also respond to a worship service that helps them understand faith as something in constant movement, being formed and reformed through personal experience along with the practices from tradition and the study of scripture. Forming faith is a process and not a destination where one reaches a point and concludes, "I now have a fully formed faith in God."

The spiritual need to journey can be equally shared between the churched and the unchurched, but, historically and traditionally, there is an emphasis on worshipers having formed faiths (e.g., in many churches, Sunday school ends in the eighth grade or when the young people are confirmed).

A worship service that invites others to stand and talk about their journeys, what they believe or are struggling to believe, and how they connect personal experiences with scripture and tradition helps others to identify and connect with these stories. The unchurched do not want to come to church to hear *the answer* to their religious and theological questions. Their fear is that worship will be an experience in having religion pushed upon them. They want to know how someone who believes arrives at the answer that makes sense for them. The more people they talk with about the answers that work for them, the more their faith is formed.

Most worship presupposes that all worshipers (members and visitors alike) are devout believers with faith formed by a religious organization. In the days of yesteryear, most visitors had been churched elsewhere, often in the same denomination. Worship was intended to enhance the formation of the worshipers' faith, not to help them embark on the journey. Doubt and disbelief were not mentioned, at least not publically. Worship could be designed to read the ancient creeds out loud because it was assumed that everyone was a believer. The premise was that everyone believed and people come to church to learn more about God. Today, we cannot design worship with that assumption. The unchurched often feel uncomfortable being asked to read the creeds when they are unsure what they believe.

After the worship service, visitors are usually invited join members for coffee and fellowship. This, too, can be uncomfortable. Members congregate with other members they know well. They want to share the news of the week and ask for prayers. The same members tend to cluster together week after week, so even the members don't always know everyone else. In numerically large congregations, members are afraid to introduce themselves to visitors because they are afraid they will offend a current member. If no one talks to the visitors and they find themselves in the corners, standing alone not quite sure what to do, they will likely look for the closest exit. Even if they liked the pastor, enjoyed the preaching and music, and felt welcomed when they walked into the sanctuary, standing alone waiting for others to approach them can be very anxiety-producing.

During coffee time, members also tend to encircle the pastor to busy him or her with the business agenda of the organization. I recommend that members not speak with the pastor after worship because they can contact the pastor at another time. The only people who should be allowed to speak to the pastor are visitors. Every member who sees a visitor should be responsible to introduce that person to the pastor and then bow out of the conversation.

A second reason not to invite an unchurched person straight to a worship service while at the same time holding invitational events is because members will measure the success of the events by how quickly the unchurched show up for church on Sunday morning. Those who are not yet involved in invitational ministry will probably continue to count (and report) how many visitors attend after an event. The team will feel pressure to produce new people in worship unless worship ceases to be the yard stick with which to assess disciple-making. Shifting this mind-set is critical. Otherwise, if the new people don't start showing up at worship, the membership may conclude that the invitational events aren't achieving the desired result. They will say things like, "I thought the point was to increase our membership," and, "Why aren't the new people coming to worship?"

It would be the unusual person who attends one or two invitational events and then accepts the organizational norm that says, "If you are a member, you show up for worship." Most unchurched people will need to attend several events before they have *any* interest in attending worship. Among those who are churched, waiting for them to show interest is an exercise in patience. However, those inside organized religion don't set the time frame between an invitational event and when someone is inspired to attend a worship service. Congregations should affirm themselves and celebrate that they are finding new ways to connect with their neighborhood and build relationships with people who are unchurched. Before they engaged in this process, they were unlikely doing so. They are making progress as long as invitational events are bringing the unchurched into the life of the congregation. For the time being, that is all that is needed. If the unchurched perceive that the congregation cares about their spiritual needs, they will eventually find their way to worship.

Seven Hospitality Guidelines for Invitational Events

To ensure that the focus is on the interests of the unchurched and that you provide an environment that makes them feel comfortable, I will offer seven hospitality guidelines for invitational events. Members need to be warm, friendly, and empathic toward the feelings of the unchurched, and intentional about for whom these events are offered. The discussion below outlines each of these hospitality guidelines and how to encourage members to honor them. The reason for the guidelines is to ensure that energy is wisely invested to achieve the desired result of spiritual and numerical growth for the congregation. Because congregations have a tendency toward morphing events into something that meets their own needs, these guidelines will increase the probability that they will offer something that appeals to people who are not churched, and will focus on practicing hospitality.

1. A member can attend an invitational event only if inviting someone to come with them.

The difference between church and invitation events is that a member can only attend an invitational event if inviting another person. I elevate this guideline to the eleventh commandment. Initially, some members will not see the reason why they can't come and not invite someone else. They will say, "I don't understand why I can't come! I have been a member of this church for twenty-five years and you are telling me I can't attend an event at my own church?" A member from the planning team needs to be able to respond, "You are more than welcome to attend. But we are holding this event to connect with the unchurched and if you come and don't bring someone, others will do so and the only ones that we will be connecting with will be those who already attend this church."

Nothing will sabotage these efforts faster than a congregation that does not honor this guideline. It only takes a few people who perceive that they should receive special status and be exempt. They may think they are entitled to an exemption because they are long-term members, hold power in the congregation, or because they "don't know anyone who is unchurched." To help them understand, the team should continually state the difference between all-church and invitational events. If the congregation has enough energy to do both at the same time, then they may plan all-church events to which members can come and not need to bring someone with them while they are also holding events that require bringing or inviting someone. Because many congregations do not have the energy to do both, however, the team may remind the members why they are holding invitational events: "As a congregation, we made the prayerful decision that God wants our church to continue and that we would be willing to do whatever it takes to make that happen. Unfortunately, that might mean sacrificing some of our own needs, e.g., fellowship events, in the process. We need to stay focused at this time because turning around the decline is God's vision for our church at this time."

Some members will make the argument that they would like to come to support the invitational event and to get to know the unchurched who will be in attendance. "This is a hospitality issue!" they will claim, and may inquire, "When will the new people have an opportunity to build relationships with the rest of the membership?" Members might feel uncomfortable about new people coming into "my church" and feeling out of the loop. They may genuinely want to extend a welcome, but they may also have a need to make sure that the new people know who they are and respect their power and status in the life of the congregation. If they have historically been given access into the inner circle of the congregation's power, the idea that those who attend these invitational events are now all getting to know each other may translate into a new inner circle emerging. The team can reassure them that there will be other opportunities for them to get to know the new people.

Hopefully, they can use their frustration and anxiety about being on the outside of the process to go out into the community and invite someone to the event so that they can attend. On Sunday morning, when they hear about all the new people who came to the event on Saturday night, that left-out feeling will motivate them to prayerfully think about who they could invite to the next event. Or, unfortunately, they may use their frustration and anxiety to cause conflict, especially if it appears that the team members are not all in agreement and willing to enforce this guideline. Some members will need more convincing than others that this is the direction that the church is moving, and, if they want to be part of the process, then what is required of them is to learn invitational skills.

If the team concedes and allows one or two people to come to an invitational event by themselves, these efforts will unravel. One exemption will break the levy for others: "If she can come and not bring someone, then why can't I?" After a while, members will stop asking and just come alone. Then, it will be the team who feels frustrated. After an event is held and evaluated, organizers will observe that what was planned to be an invitational event ended up being an all-church event because the only ones in attendance were members. When this tends to happen, the process comes to an abrupt end because the desired result of the events is not being achieved. One or two invitational events that morph into all-church events lead the team to conclude, "These invitational events aren't working at our church. We are not going to do them anymore!"

2. Members talk with the unchurched, not with other members.

Another important reason why members cannot attend an invitational event is: if the number of members significantly outweighs the number of unchurched, then the unchurched may be the ones who feel like outsiders. The more church people at an event, the stronger the tendency will be for them to interact with each other instead of with the unchurched. A brief comment turns into a lengthy conversation between two members. Or the opposite happens: too many church people "pounce" on the unchurched and they feel overwhelmed. The unchurched only need to meet a few people to feel connected to the membership and to talk about their spiritual needs. It is more important for them to feel this emotional connection with a few people than to meet and shake hands with everyone who is attending the invitational event.

3. Members are honest about why they are inviting people.

The third guideline is that the congregation is transparent about why it is holding invitational events. The neighborhood will wonder why a congregation wakes up one day and decides that it wants to reconnect. They will assume that the congregation is motivated by money (which is why invitational events do not cost). The unchurched are on guard about this being the reason, and so the event actually has to work toward proving otherwise. They assume that the reason is money until someone articulates something different to them. If nothing is said, then they will assume that the church is doing a membership drive to increase their annual budget. Rather, the congregation needs to communicate that it cares about the community and their formation of faith.

Doing the exercises on framing invitations in chapter 6 will help members identify a theological reason why they are reaching out to the community. Everyone needs to be saying the same thing, as the neighborhood will begin comparing notes: "One friend told me that they were reaching out for this reason, but another friend told me that it was really about money." The framing of this reason doesn't have to sound theological, but it needs to place the emphasis on how the people being invited will benefit and not sound self-serving or selfish on the part of the congregation. For instance, a congregation may say something like, "We feel God calling us to increase our ministries and help people form their faith in new ways, and so we are trying to talk to as many people in our neighborhood as possible so that we can discern their spiritual needs." I have heard some congregations say, "If the way we worship is not working for people in our neighborhood, we want to explore what other forms of worship might be more appealing, and we figure the way to find this out is to start talking to people."

4. Members invite only those who are not going to any church.

Reaching out to the already-churched can create a new set of problems. There will be those who are easily attracted from their current congregation because they are upset about something happening there. If they are resistant to change, they may think that attending another church is a way not to have to deal with their anxiety or to assert pressure on their own church not to implement change. Chances are, after time, they will become resistant to some of the changes being made in there new congregation, too. What members should do is help these people adapt to the change in their own congregation rather than offer them an escape route. Congregations that warmly welcome disgruntled members from their sister congregations risk being devalued in the eyes of their colleagues in Christ. "Sheep stealing" from other congregations is not what Jesus commissions us to do. In this circumstance, you are not making disciples, you are only shifting them from one congregation to another.

"Can I invite someone who hasn't been to church for a while?" Several authors have noted that there is little difference in the thinking about church between the unchurched and the dechurched; both tend to perceive that the church is not meeting their spiritual needs. The length of time since people have been active in a congregation and the reasons why they became inactive may determine whether they should be invited back to this church or helped to find another.

Congregations often express interest in trying to get the dechurched to return to the worship service. I refer to this process as "activating the inactive." If the congregation feels really passionate about trying to do this, then I suggest that two people from the congregation pay the dechurched a visit and have a conversation about why he or she left and what would be needed in his or her spiritual formation to return. However, studies prove this is not an effective way to numerically grow a congregation and it does not honor Jesus' commission to make disciples. We can assume that dechurched persons have had plenty of opportunity to form their faith and invite others. If they don't want to come to church, then it is unlikely that they will feel inspired to invite someone else. I suggest that members undertake this process only if it will create momentum for reaching out to the unchurched. Some congregations need to feel successful before they are willing to reach out to their mission field. The risk is that, if the congregation perceives that activating the inactive is not productive, they may not be able to access the energy needed to invite the unchurched.

5. One member can only bring one person.

Another guideline is that one member should bring one unchurched person to one invitational event. If a member brings two people, it should be a couple. Ideally, a couple in the congregation would invite another couple. This guideline assures that those invited will have someone attending to their hospitality needs. By inviting one person, the invitational minister can introduce that person to a few others, assessing how comfortable the person seems with meeting these new people. The objective is not to get the unchurched person to shake hands with as many people as possible, but to have one or two meaningful interactions. An unchurched person should meet churched *and* other unchurched people. By inviting only one person to one event, the invitational minister can constantly be aware of what the person is doing, with whom the person is speaking, and whether the person needs immediate support or guidance.

6. The first few events should be held in neutral space, not on church property.

The first few events should be large-scale, low interactive events held off campus. The unchurched often express feeling uncomfortable being in a religious organization. A neutral space breaks down the barrier between who is "in" and who is "out." Neutral space plays down the designations of host and guest. A congregation should make sure that everyone who attends from the community understands that this event is sponsored by them and that they are willing to leave the comfort of their own property. Congregations have held great events in the community and, because they did not let everyone know that they had planned the event, the perception among the community was that the cultural council or another community group held it. A banner hung between trees with the church's name, handing out brochures, and the pastor working the crowd introducing him- or herself lets people know that this is an invitational event sponsored by the church.

Town squares, parks, lakeside areas, and community centers create an environment for getting to know others in a relaxed atmosphere. Settings in nature, especially at the peak of a season's beauty, often help people feel spiritual, thus connecting that feeling with a religious organization. Some communities require permits for a church to use public land. If the governing board in the community is hesitant about granting the permit (and make sure they are invited as well), then the planning team may need to make a presentation to them that differentiates an invitational event from a worship service. Most communities are reluctant to allow churches access to "liturgical use of town property." Their fear is that the churched will be evangelizing people in the park. If the event is designed as a family one, open to everyone in the community, most communities will be supportive because the event is something that benefits the whole community.

A large interactive event such as a concert works well as one of the first invitational events. Inviting people who are unchurched to a concert helps them to anticipate what will be expected from them (versus worship, where it is less easy to anticipate expectations). Concerts are fun, especially in the summer on a field, where everyone brings a lawn chair. The planning team needs to select music that will appeal to the age ranges and cultural groupings they hope to attract. A cookout before the concert in the church parking lot may be coupled with this event and is more interactive than the concert. This may give some people an opportunity to briefly have a conversation with others before the concert. If the event is on the low side of the interactive scale, sometimes it's good to plan a slightly higher level of interaction for a limited time frame before or after. It is possible to hold an event that is so low interactive that no one acknowledges the presence of another (e.g., an event in a movie theatre).

7. Plan events in a sequence.

Planning teams will design a sequence of events in which one member will invite the same unchurched person from one to the next. The premise is that the unchurched person needs time to develop relationships with others. This person is trying to make a decision about whether he or she wants to invest emotional energy into getting to know these particular people. It takes more than one event to build a relationship. A low interactive event such as ballroom dancing may be fun and may introduce people to one another, but is not enough to convince most people to share their faith. If I show up at a baseball game and meet a few church people, I am not ready to sign up for church membership. It will take a number of invitational events, in a carefully planned sequence.

So that the unchurched can make the decision that they are interested in attending, events should be planned in sequence, moving from large or small scale and low interactive to small scale and high interactive. Worship can be an example of a large-scale, high interactive event, depending on the forms that comprise the worship service. A member who stands before the congregation and shares his or her personal experience of God is a high interactive form of worship. Interestingly, the higher interactive worship is, the more it appeals to the unchurched. Traditional worship tends to be low interactive. If the unchurched are seeking opportunities for high interaction with others, then inviting them to worship may not meet their spiritual needs. Small group sharing may be more conducive to meeting their spiritual needs.

Members should be reminded that the sequence is not to invite someone to a high interactive event and then invite them to a low interactive worship service. To do so would be out of sequence. Inviting someone unchurched to a high interactive event such as a small group and then to a low interactive one will make them wonder if "the church is just trying to get me into their membership and ask me to pledge." If they are seeking a high interactive opportunity, then getting them to attend a low interactive worship service will make them suspicious that the congregation has an agenda that does not prioritize meeting their spiritual needs. Leaders need to emphasize that the unchurched are seeking high interactive opportunities; that they want to have a place to come to share their faith. While they may not feel comfortable doing this in their first few interactions with church members, the hope is that their spiritual formation could be assisted by attending worship, but that may depend on getting to know them so that you will know what changes need to be made before you invite them.

The next event, then, moves along the continuum from low interactive to high interactive, although not immediately. There should be a number of different events in between. The goal of the first event is to provide an atmosphere of interest so that someone who is unchurched will want to be invited to a second event. Thus, two invitational events are being planned simultaneously. The second event is announced at the first event and should be related in terms of interest. The second event should be similar to the event being attended. For instance, if you hold a classic rock concert, do not advertise that your next concert will be with an alternative punk rock group. There should be some loose thread that weaves one event to the next. For instance, after a classic rock concert, a congregation might hold a game night at the church for "Name that Tune" with music from the '60s and '70s. If people came because they were interested in the first event, a similar event will likely interest them enough to return.

The progression from low to high interactive also allows for moving from community space to the church building and then back out into the community. Small group sharing in members' homes may be a better alternative than in the ladies parlor. Groups should be comprised of between six and twelve people so that one or two people do not dominate the conversation. Leaders may offer a sign-up sheet or ask individual members to invite specific people. Those who were invited by a church member may now be placed in a group with other church members, and not necessarily with the specific church member who invited them. It may also be helpful to equip facilitators for the small group discussion, perhaps with a selection of questions that serve to generate conversation (and reduce everyone's anxiety level).

Guiding Force for All-Church Tasks

Invitational ministry and its goals become the guiding force for all other tasks. No committee or team takes on a task that does not contribute to the mission of making disciples. The pastor continues to provide pastoral care, but focuses more of his or her energy to equip others for the ministries of caring and invitation. The treasurer continues to pay the bills to practice good stewardship. The finance team doesn't need to micromanage spending for fear that the money will run out. The outreach team continues to plan the annual picnic by the lake, as long as it is planned as an activity to which members invite others who are unchurched. If the Christian education team sponsors a yearly celebration for its teachers, they can still hold this event; but it must be tweaked to have something to do with invitational ministry. (Perhaps introduce the parents in the neighborhood to the Sunday school teachers and publically affirm their gifts and talents of working with the children.) Activities that are enjoyed as a congregation continue to be held as long as they are tweaked to be activities in the service of making disciples.

Numerically growing congregations prioritize invitational ministry as the centerpiece of their ministry. It becomes the most important ministry in the life of their congregation at this moment in the church's history. Once embedded in the organization's culture, the congregation will then be ready to turn its attention to other tasks. Congregations that navigate through this wilderness present invitational ministry as the first fruit in their discipleship. In other words, if members perceive that they only have so much energy to invest, they invest it in work that they believe that Jesus commissions them to do. They do not continue to exclusively invest their energy in ministries that solely attend to the spiritual needs of the current membership. Invitational ministry requires every member to invest this energy, because much is needed. The harvest is plentiful and the laborers are few. Invitational ministry should not get the leftover energy after the needs of the organization have been sufficiently met. Jesus asks us for our very best effort to invest energy into the mission of making disciples.

Chapter 5

Planning Invitational Events

The success of an invitational event is predetermined before the event is held. Congregations that plan an event and then take a "wait and see how this works" attitude are usually in for disappointment. The process of planning and evaluating events should produce the insight that events need to be intentionally planned out to ensure success. This is so critical because it is the way to access spiritual energy in a congregation. A well-planned event that everyone perceives is successful builds momentum, creates energy, and feels exciting. Those in the congregation who sit on the sidelines and watch what is unfolding before they decide whether or not to get involved will get caught up in the excitement and participate when they can see that the efforts are producing the desired result. Congregational members who perceive the energy invested is coming back to them tenfold feel good about themselves, their church, and their relationship with God in Jesus.

In the last chapter, I emphasized the difference between all-church events, when everyone in the congregation is welcome to attend and inviting an unchurched person is optional, and invitational events, when only those members who invite an unchurched person may attend. The seven guidelines provide the structure for invitational events. Now we turn to a discussion about planning, equally important. This chapter will explore each of the six phases of planning: (1) selecting the team, (2) determining goals, (3) discerning a vision, (4) generating ideas, (5) decision-making, and (6) evaluating the success of the event.

The ability to plan an event is a skill that invitational ministers will need to learn. One exercise I have the team do is to plan three invitational events that they will *not* implement. Therefore, they have access to unlimited money, members, and resources to plan the event. They don't have to listen to, "We don't have enough money to do that!" The team can have fun imagining the possibilities from a mind-set of abundance rather than allow this fear of scarcity to restrain them. By practicing skills such as brainstorming new ideas and beyond-the-box thinking, they are free to be innovative and creative. Developing strategic skills challenges the usual obstacles that sabotage a good idea. Church floors are littered with good ideas that were never implemented because when they were suggested, everyone else was trying to figure out why they wouldn't work. While planning invitational events will feel labor-intensive, learning new skills for invitational ministry sets the stage for successful invitational events.

Selecting the Team

Depending on the congregation's size, multiple teams may be commissioned to plan multiple invitational events. Ideally, one team plans one event, with perhaps a few members being on the second team to ensure some consistency in planning one event and then the other. The second event should be similar to the first event with respect to interest so that those who showed interest in the first event are likely to show interest in the second. A few team members who helped plan the first event will transition to help plan the second event so that they can share with the second team what the first team was thinking. Because the second event will be announced at the first event, and so forth, two events are always being planned at the same time. But if a congregation does not have enough people initially to form two teams, then one team will be planning two events.

The place to begin is in the careful selection of the team for the planning phases. The pastor should not stand at the pulpit and ask for volunteers. This way of getting people on a team assumes that no skills are needed, only interest in being on a team. People volunteer for various reasons, not all are because they want to be helpful to the process. Some just want to make sure that their power and status in the life of the congregation will be preserved through the process. Asking for volunteers gives the impression that people don't want to do something, and you are just hoping that people will come forward. To ask for volunteers may send the message that the congregation is in short supply of energy. Rather, the pastor and leaders want to create the perception that it is an honor to be asked to be on the team, because they have identified that certain members have the potential to learn new skills that the body of Christ needs to make disciples of the unchurched.

When energy is in short supply, most pastors and leaders are grateful for anyone who wants to be on a team. A congregation that begins this process from a perception of scarcity runs the risk of emphasizing that perception rather than the perception of abundance, which creates energy. I think that the most debilitating factor in mainline decline is the underutilization of the gifts of people already sitting in our pews. The challenge is to link ministry with minister and develop the skills that each minister needs to do a particular ministry. Mismatching ministries with ministers leads to a lack of energy in a congregation because people are not matched by their passions but by whatever opportunity presented itself at the time they felt like they wanted to participate. So, the first needed skills are developed among pastors and leaders who can recognize the skills in others.

Who should not be on the team? The strategic thinking that we want our enemies closer than our friends translates into church life when we put the members who tend to be the most resistant on a planning team. While initially this may appear to be a good move, the problem arises when they oppose new ideas before they are developed. Their negativity may discourage other team members from feeling the freedom to brainstorm beyond-the-box, because the fear of scarcity often underlies resistance. I hear members say, "I gave up offering new ideas, because I felt like every time I opened my mouth, the idea was shot down before I even got it out." The momentum the team will generate will increase and will help redirect the energy from resistance as long as they function as one. Often a team thinks they need someone to play the devil's advocate so that they can see things from a different perspective or anticipate resistance. But the team doesn't need to navigate around resistance, only to build momentum to redirect any negative energy.

Adapting to change is a skill that team members have already developed or are willing to learn. Invitational ministry embodies a skill of adapting well to change. The congregation is about to change dramatically in terms of membership, perhaps ethnic composition, as it embraces new people. New people come with new ideas. Some leaders think that putting those who are resistant to change on a team and empowering them with decision-making will make them more flexible to change. This isn't always the case. I've seen members who helped make the decision turn around and orchestrate a group of people to resist that very decision from being implemented. Putting resistant church members on a team may grant them a front row seat to hold the congregation hostage from making the changes needed for invitational ministry.

The following offers a list of criteria for the selection of a team member.

- A member who is able to articulate his or her faith in such a way that encourages others to do so.
- A member who has expressed interest in getting to know the neighbors rather than fear regarding what will become of the church. The team needs members who are love-driven toward meeting the spiritual needs of their neighbors, not fear-driven and obsessed about the future of the church.
- A member who has planned other events, activities, programs, or capital campaigns and does not suggest quick fixes, but is willing to wrestle with tough issues until something of value emerges.
- A member who is not afraid to try new ways of being and doing church, is willing to take risks, and can view a series of failures as steps toward success.
- A member who can identify gifts and skills in others and has the ability to ask people to use these gifts/skills in ways that build confidence.
- A member who has, on other occasions, suggested turning to prayer when the congregation has hit a road block.

- A member who has confronted his or her own prejudices and realizes the benefits of gathering a multicultural community; a member who agrees with the idea that "whomever God has placed in this community is God's gift to the future of this congregation."
- A member who is excited about inviting others and perhaps has done so in the past; a member who realizes that the bus filled with new young people is not coming—instead, the congregation needs to hire its own bus to go out into the community.
- A member who interacts regularly with the unchurched and would feel comfortable inviting a few of these people to a planning team meeting so that they could help the congregation with this mission.
- A member who has been generous with his or her time, money, and talents, but has not crossed into a relational pattern of addiction through over-volunteerism within the congregation.
- A member who is not afraid of conflict but is able to expand the pie rather than shift to the default positions of compromise and accommodation.
- A member who wants to engage in invitational ministry because he or she feels called to it, and not because he or she perceives it is a solution to financial problems.

Teams should be composed of eight to twelve people—small enough that every member has input, and large enough to reduce the risk that one or two people will dominate the discussion or become the decision makers whose power convinces others. The composition of the team should also be a cross-sectional representation of the entire congregation. This diversity encourages the team to widen its view. Ideally, the team might invite a few unchurched friends and family members to some of the planning sessions, to make sure that the team's efforts are focusing on what will appeal to the unchurched. For example, a congregation hoping to appeal to young families should have at least one unchurched parent on the planning team. Most unchurched people are happy to help as long as they feel that the team genuinely is seeking their opinions and perspective, and they don't perceive their inclusion as a ploy to get them to come to a worship service.

Invitational ministry involves a set of skills, and these skills are relational. The team, then, should set aside time to build relationships with each other, *even if* they are already acquainted. The team will be planning events that help people build relationships on a deeper level. As they engage in this process themselves, they will learn how to help others go about doing this. Team members will need to learn to express feelings and thoughts in an open manner. They will learn to speak openly about their faith and to articulate that faith to the congregation. Planning an invitational event should be considered a Christian practice, as it helps people become more connected to the way that Jesus works through them to minister to others. The following are some facilitating questions that may help the team to reach this level of sharing.

- Why do you believe that God has called you to be a member on this team?
- What do you have to offer to the process of planning invitational events that perhaps no other member has to offer?
- Which of your gifts, talents, and skills will be useful to the planning process?
- What skills do you hope to learn along the way? Are these skills transferable to other settings, such as family relationships and work?
- What happens when you feel anxious? How to you manage anxiety? Are you able to express your feelings openly, or do you tend to wait until someone else acknowledges them?
- How will you handle yourself when you are convinced that you are right?
- How willingly do you affirm others? Are you willing to let others know when you think they have a good idea? When others are suggesting a good idea, are you thinking about how you can expand on the idea, or why the idea won't work?
- What will it be like for you to begin inviting friends and family to the church? Are there some aspects of the church

that you feel ashamed about? Can you share that with other team members?

- Are you a hopeful person? How do you envision the future of the congregation at this point in the process? When you feel discouraged, does that invoke "all or nothing" thinking?
- At what point in the process will it be important to you that the team turns to prayer?

These relationship-building exercises help members feel more emotionally connected to each other. They also help the team to know who does what well and who needs to learn which relational skills. One of the biggest challenges for the team is being able to identify who already possesses the skill for a certain task and who needs guidance to develop that skill. Past behavior is a good indicator of future behavior. If the team has witnessed one member demonstrating a skill on another mission project, it is likely that person will be able to do that task again. Keep in mind that the church is in the business of changing people's lives, and needs to provide opportunities for team members to learn new skills so that they benefit from being on the team. The idea is to balance the opportunity to use one's already acquired skills with learning new skills by practicing.

One of the major differences between a committee and a team is that a committee does all the work, while a team coordinates the work and then delegates the responsibility to those who already possess the skills, and teaches those skills to those who are willing to learn. Because I am proposing that you use teams and not committees, the team members will discern what needs to be done, who is likely to be able to accomplish these tasks, and who needs to be equipped to do new tasks. The pastor tends to know who already has which skills and gifts, and he or she may serve in a consulting role, helping the team members match skills with ministers. Given that many congregations have operated with a committee model for years, teams may initially need to resist the temptation to function like a committee. The challenge comes when a team member perceives that it is easier to do the task "by myself" than to equip someone else to do it. They may also need to resist committee thinking that says, "I can do it better than others," rather than equipping someone else to do it. Teams need to continually remind themselves that they are transforming members into disciples as well as changing the lives of the unchurched.

The first invitational event is critical in setting the stage for a second. Team members are excited about this new venture. They are hopeful, and are willing to invest energy into planning and implementing. The first invitational event must be perceived as successful by those who are involved in the event as well as by the members who sit on the sidelines to pass judgment upon whether invitational events are going to work toward numerical church growth. To be excited and hopeful, and then to have that energy deflated because it is perceived that the effort failed is not a path most congregations will be able to walk.

The perception of success is derived from expectations. If expectations are too high, the team will have to overcome that mental chart in members' minds that defines success. Instead, the team should be the ones to define success, and, therefore, define what the congregation can expect from the first invitational event. Expectations from the congregation will tend to be unrealistic. Members will assume that one invitational event will get hundreds of people from the neighborhood to be interested in the church. That won't happen. Rather, depending on the size of the congregation, the expectation that eight to twelve members will invite eight to twelve unchurched people is what will define success.

So the team's challenge for the first invitational event is to make sure that eight to twelve people who are unchurched will be present. One of the best ways to make sure this happens is for the team members themselves to be the invitational ministers at the first event, modeling for other members this new practice. If there are eight to twelve team members and each one brings an unchurched person, then the event will be perceived as successful if this number was determined to be the goal. Because others cannot come to the event unless they bring someone who is unchurched, the first activity may need to be planned as a small-scale, low interactive one. Members who hear through the grapevine that the event was successful may be more likely to invite someone to the next event.

The consequences of not inviting an unchurched person to an event or inviting a person who is churched elsewhere should be grounds for resignation or dismissal from the team. If team members accept excuses from one another, it will be easy to accept excuses from members of the congregation (who will undoubtedly offer them). Thus, the requirement for being on a team is to invite someone who is unchurched to the event being planned. The requirement for remaining on a team is having followed through by actually bringing someone unchurched to the event. While "life happens," the team should not tolerate any excuses. Once a team member models that one can attend an event and not bring someone who is unchurched, others in the congregation will follow accordingly.

Determining Goals

The goal of an invitational event is not numerical church growth, nor counting the people who come to the event. There are two goals: (1) to transition members into being disciples and (2) to transition the unchurched into being disciples. The team should keep record of how many of the unchurched are attending invitational events for the purpose of assessing whether or not the events being offered are attractive to the unchurched, but not for the purpose of numerical membership growth. Being invited to a church and doing the inviting is the beginning of the journey into discipleship. Disciples are made by forming faith through Christian practices. Invitational ministry is the practice through which people's lives are changed as they transition into this process.

I suggest that two indicators of discipleship-making are counted. One, the team should track how many members are inviting the unchurched to an invitational event. This helps them to know if the exercises on framing invitations and equipping members to manage their anxiety and feel more confident are making a difference. If members are not yet taking the plunge and inviting the unchurched, that might inform the team that more exercises are needed to move in this direction. Changing people's behavior is not easy, and the team should count so that they can assess where the congregation is in terms of its ability to transition from behaving like members to like disciples who practice invitational ministry.

Two, the team should count how many of the unchurched are coming to invitational events. This gives the team information about whether the events are attractive or interesting to the unchurched. Teams who record this information over time can tell which events tend to draw the most unchurched and which do not. These numbers can be helpful to the next few teams as they plan events. Counting how many of the unchurched attend programs that address concerns of the community also reveals what the community is concerned about so that the congregation can pray about how to take appropriate action to help.

If, for denominational records, a congregation is required to count how many people attend worship, then that number should continue to be recorded, but it is not a reliable indicator of how many members are becoming disciples. Some churches also continue to count membership, which is probably the least accurate indicator of faith formation. Congregations only tend to "clean up the rolls" when they are in transition for new pastoral leadership or are looking at ways to reduce their expenditures if they pay a set fee per member to their denominational body. These numbers are often so skewed that a congregation doesn't really know how many people are connected with their church. In some communities and among some ethnicities, "joining" is not something that they would do, but they would show up for worship every Sunday.

I would not suggest that the team make public their findings regarding these two numbers. Members would be excited to see little dots on a graph that show new people are coming to their church, but the unchurched may see this chart in the fellowship hall as confirming their fear that the congregation is only interested in new members and their money. Most members will observe the new people at the invitational events, while there will always be members who only attend worship and, when the new people are not coming to worship, express their concern that "invitational events are not working because the new people are not coming to worship." The teams will have to work hard to overcome this expectation. Reporting on the number who find their way to worship is likely to halt momentum for planning additional invitational events.

Discerning a Vision and Writing a Vision Statement

A vision is a picture of how your church will look once goals are reached. Seeing that your goal is to make disciples, you might imagine a congregation filled with people excited about their relationship with Jesus Christ. A vision statement for a multicultural congregation embraces individuals with respect for gender, age, race/ethnicity, sexual orientation, economic circumstance, and ability.[1] The vision statement may project an image of what a congregation would look like while joyfully worshiping and sharing cultural traditions. The purpose of casting a vision is to create hope, which energizes people to try new practices such as invitational ministry.

Congregations get lost in the journey when they are afraid to imagine the possibilities. They may borrow someone else's vision statement that isn't relevant for their own situation, or they can't think of anything so they skim over this part of the process. Everyone works feverishly, but no one knows which direction they are heading. What tends to happen is that every member is doing his or her own thing, and no synergy is generated by working together. Every congregation has more than enough energy to reach out to its community as long as it works as a team, heading toward the same vision.

A vision statement should be about two to five sentences in length and create a visual image. A longer statement reduces the likelihood that members will be able to recite it from memory, share it with others in the community, and remember it long enough to be able to live it out. A vision statement that is too long will end up in a file cabinet. To make committing the vision statement to memory easier, artwork may be produced to visually reinforce what the congregation is hoping to achieve. Paintings, fiber art such as pictorial quilts, photography, and sculptures all lend themselves to this purpose. An artist may actually create the visual during the worship service itself. The artist's creation may remain in the sanctuary during the time that the congregation is transitioning toward becoming disciples.

The content of the statement should be theological. It should state what the congregation believes that its ministry is to this particular community. Too many vision statements can be summarized as, "This is how we take care of ourselves." An inward-focused statement does not create hope or energy for the future; vision statements that make no mention about the congregation's ministry to the neighborhood are doomed to be shelved. Instead of creating hope and momentum, these statements may actually have the opposite effect, producing despair and stagnation.

A vision statement seeks to keep the congregation focused and hopeful about its future. When congregations become depressed, they tend to adopt a subconscious mission statement: remain open for next week's worship service. Few people are going to want to be part of a congregation that doesn't feel good about themselves or their ministry, so strive to make the vision statement upbeat and inspirational. A visitor should have the response, "Wow, I want to be a part of this organization!"

To construct a vision statement, the following may be prayerfully considered:

- What has been the congregation's vision of the church in the past? Was that vision realized?
- What plagues has God recently sent to your church to try to soften your congregation's heart? (Revisit the exodus story, casting the church as Egypt.)
- Why did God put your church in this particular community? Why do you believe that God wants this congregation to continue to be a church in this particular community?
- What gifts/talents do members of your congregation possess that may be of service to this community?
- What gifts/talents/skills might your members need to learn to meet the spiritual needs of your community?

The following exercise may also help a congregation to discern vision. For those who are able, the team can lead a congregation on a hiking trip up a mountain (or find a hill accessible by wheelchair or take an elevator or stairs to the top of a tall building; be creative). At the summit, ask people to imagine what God is revealing to them about the Promised Land. Leaders may read biblical passages about what God has revealed in the past, as assurance and hope that God will reveal new visions for the church of today. This exercise reminds people that the congregation is the congregation with or without its sanctuary space or church building. The vision may be that the congregation should sell its building and be a congregation out in the community or a congregation without walls. Taking people to a place they do not usually wander may help them to see themselves and their congregation in a new light. The team can encourage them to share what they imagined through this experience to begin to construct a vision narrative.

The following are some examples of vision statements that help move congregations from membership to discipleship.

- We believe that God calls us to reach out to our neighborhood by creating opportunities for conversation with people who are not churched. We regularly hold events and every member of our congregation personally invites someone who is not affiliated with a religious community. These events help us to build relationships with all of our brothers and sisters in Christ.
- We believe that in the kingdom of God all people will gather together and worship Jesus. Instead of waiting for our neighborhood to become more ethnically diverse, we believe that we should be more intentional about inviting others and gathering together people of diversity in our congregation. As people learn how to relate to others, then our neighborhoods will also become more ethnically diverse. We believe that the church should be a forerunner in this process.
- Our ministry is to people who are not yet Christian. The church is not in the "business" of keeping those who are already disciples happy and content, but to challenge them to make disciples of those in our neighborhood. We believe our reason for existence is to help others find their way into the Christian faith. We believe that those who are unchurched just need a positive experience of being around those who are Christian.

The visioning process can create excitement about invitational ministry, or it may lead the congregation to consider other options, discussed previously. Either way, prayerfully considering what God is calling the congregation to do should be a core practice of any church.

Generating Ideas for Invitational Events

Team members should begin the process of generating ideas for invitational events by gathering in a sacred place for prayer.

Silent prayer and meditation gives God a chance to speak to the team, revealing aspects of a good idea to each member, like puzzle pieces. What God does not tend to do is reveal the whole idea to one person and then reveal nothing to anyone else on the team. This time of silent prayer to hear God speak may be followed by members of the team praying for each other, preparing to listen actively before speaking–perhaps implementing the three-second guideline of silence before they speak, so that they are not thinking about what they will say while another person is speaking. They may also pray for each other's personal concerns so that team members are building relationships that are deeper than friendships–thus, doing what they are equipping the membership to be able to do.

Each team member will have a piece of the puzzle that, when put together, promises a good idea for an invitational event. The only way to put that puzzle together is for the team to have a conversation in which each team member contributes to the idea. Those who do not feel comfortable contributing their part of the idea, or who are often passed over in favor of someone who speaks without allowing others to get a word in, may have the corner piece that will frame the idea and give it life.

The approach I am suggesting is much different from the way most teams tend to generate ideas. What they often tend to do is encourage one person to suggest one idea, and then another person suggest another idea. The premise is that each person may have an idea that is fully formed, and that others will weigh it as either a good one or a not-likely-to-work one. The team listens to everyone pitch their own ideas and then tries to determine which idea should be implemented. Often, the criteria for decision-making is lowest cost, how easy the event is to plan in terms of their own energy, and/or some other unarticulated criteria.

We have a natural tendency to fuse ideas with people. When an idea is suggested by someone who is well liked and respected by the rest of the congregation, the team may perceive that the idea is good and is likely to be supportive because this member was the one who suggested it. Conversely, some may think that the idea is not likely to work, but they may not feel comfortable saying so because of this team member's status in congregational life, and so they don't put their hearts and souls into implementing it.

Another potential problem is that the member who suggests the idea now "owns" that idea and may have an emotional investment in making sure that the idea will work (even if it is unlikely to do so). This person's passion to support his or her own idea becomes stronger than the potential for the idea to achieve the desired result. When the idea does not bring the desired result, the member may be angry at others who he or she perceives did not support it by putting energy into it (which may be an accurate reflection of the situation).

When two members both think they have a good idea, the ideas have to compete for attention from the team, and acceptance by its members. If the idea is fused with the person, then it can seem as if the two people are each competing to have his or her idea chosen to be turned into an event. Which idea wins and which idea loses may be determined by which member is more well-liked, has been a member longer, has more power in the congregation, or is more likely to influence others to see things his or her way. The focus is on which team member will "win" by having the team choose his or her idea over the other. When this situation arises, the usual consequence is that the team loses because it selects an idea for reasons other than its potential for bringing the unchurched to an invitational event.

Another possible scenario is that an idea will be suggested that no one on the team seems to hear. Perhaps the idea comes from someone new to the congregation or an unchurched person that others just met during the meeting. Team members may not "hear" a good idea because they are resentful that it was suggested by someone perceived as an outsider or someone who is not supporting the church financially. When pastors suggest ideas, they tend to fall flat, but if allowed to circulate for awhile in members' minds, tend to resurface through the suggestion of a member. If the pastor is on the team, he or she should function more as a facilitator or process consultant to point out when ideas are becoming attached to people and offer leadership to allow ideas to develop and be owned by the team rather than by certain individuals.

An exercise that is helpful to generate ideas begins with prayer. Someone will verbally suggest an idea that this person believes God has revealed. If only a piece of the puzzle, then the assumption is that others have other pieces of the idea. So beginning with the person sitting next to the person who suggested the idea, every member of the team goes around the table, embellishing the same idea, until it is developed. No one is allowed to evaluate an underdeveloped idea by saying it's crazy or will never work, because it is too early to reach that conclusion. The premise in this exercise is that every idea holds potential as long as it is invested with energy and allowed time to be developed. In this light, there are no bad ideas, only underdeveloped ideas. Often, the most far-reaching, seemingly impossible idea generates the most creativity and enthusiasm. The team might have to work harder to see how one idea might hold potential, but, in so doing, they may depend more upon the wisdom and guidance of Jesus.

Because every team member contributed to the original idea, the team (and not any individual member) now owns the idea and has an equal investment in implementing the idea as an invitational event as well as ensuring its success. Ideally, by the time that the idea is put into practice, no one can remember who initially suggested the idea. Several ideas should come to the surface so that they can be assessed in terms of which has the most potential.

Decision-Making

How does a team assess whether an idea is likely to help reach the goal? The following additional criteria should help your team make this decision:

1. An idea is likely to work if it has been done in the recent past (five years ago or less) *and* produced the desired result. Remember, just because something has been done previously doesn't mean that a team evaluated its effectiveness and concluded that it was a success. Too often, the team is relieved to do something that has been tried before so "we don't have to reinvent the wheel." They may recall how people from the congregation turned out to support the event, but they are not remembering that few members invited the unchurched, or that the unchurched did not come on their own.

2. Likewise, the team should not revert to events done in the past that *raised a lot of money,* so that the event is *remembered* as successful. The team members should check in with others

about the outcome of each event that the congregation has held in the past and evaluate whether that outcome is in line with their current goal. Success is measured differently for each event depending on the goal.

3. Just because an event worked in the past and brought the unchurched into the building doesn't necessarily mean that this event will produce that same result twenty years later. Events have a shelf life. For instance, years ago New England congregations used to hold ham and bean suppers, and everyone in the community showed up for dinner on Friday night. Few people would go to a ham and bean supper today. If we want to reach the next generation, we have to serve something different for dinner.

4. Teams may rush to reject an idea because when they held that event in the past it did not bring people back for Sunday morning worship. The event may have held *potential* to attract people back for *another* invitational event, but that first event was meant at the time to be a "one-time" event held to transition people *directly* from no church involvement to signing on the dotted line of membership.

5. An idea is likely to work if another congregation in the neighborhood is experiencing some success with it and the mission field reflects similar demographics. I am not suggesting congregations copy what other congregations are doing, but researching what other congregations are doing increases the chances of an idea holding potential. Most numerically growing congregations are happy to help declining congregations with new ideas and/or with the implementation of those ideas. They are often honored to be asked to help. Congregations in decline often perceive that they are competing for a small, limited number of people. Numerically growing congregations tend to be more aware of the high percentage of people in their community who are unchurched and perceive that if churches work together, they are more likely to all benefit by creating a culture in which attending a religious organization is the norm within their community.

If a group of people in the church becomes fixated on an idea as "the only way to save the church," then the idea should be abandoned for the time being. Too much pressure on the success of an event may cause team members to put too much emotional investment into the event. This raises everyone's anxiety. The congregation should look forward to the event as a way to begin the process of living out God's vision to make disciples, and not as a desperate attempt to prevent drowning. Functioning in panic mode leads congregations to make fatal decisions. They become more anxious, deeper in their depression, and less hopeful about their future. This is not the feeling that you want to project into the community.

Once the team thinks an idea holds potential and is in line with God's vision for the church, they will need to decide how to announce the idea to the congregation. If the pastor makes the announcement, it may appear to be the pastor's idea or that the pastor is "pushing" these invitational events upon the congregation. On the other hand, if the pastor does not announce the invitational event, it looks like he or she doesn't know what is going on (so the pastor can't win!). Ask someone from the team to stand before the congregation during a worship service and say, "After much prayerful discernment, we believe that God has blessed us with this idea for an invitational event." The pastor may follow up the announcement about the invitational event with an announcement about the first workshop on how to frame an invitation. This way the congregation understands that the pastor's role is to equip disciples for invitational ministry (and he or she should be announcing that they also will be bringing an unchurched person to the invitational event) and that he or she supports what the team is doing to provide a venue for the invitational ministers to practice their skills.

During this announcement, it should be made *very* clear that only those who will be inviting someone who is unchurched are invited to attend the event. If the event costs, then the invitational minister will purchase one ticket for themselves and one ticket for the unchurched person they have invited. Tickets should be made available before the event, and preferably in the congregation's gathering space for fellowship. Asking invitational ministers to buy tickets serves a number of purposes. First, the team can be better prepared because they know how many people to expect. Second, the details of the event can be printed on the ticket as a reminder to the unchurched invitees. Third, people are less likely to bow out at the last minute simply because they are tired or feel anxious if they know that the invitational minister has bought a ticket for them to attend.

Collecting Information and Hospitality

During the event, the team should make sure that they ask for everyone's e-mail addresses and/or cell phone numbers (to send a text message), but don't make it mandatory, as some may perceive this as too invasive. (See the following paragraph for specifics on dealing with such concerns.) Similar to the pads in the pews that are passed from one worshiper to the next to collect information and be hospitable, or a guest book for visitors to sign before they leave, events should also include gathering contact information. This should be done at the beginning, as people are coming into the event venue rather than afterward, when some people may not want to take the time to do this because they are tired and ready to go home. The team should collect contact information from *both* the churched and the unchurched, so that the unchurched don't feel singled out. An additional benefit is that the team will note which members are becoming invitational ministers.

The team member providing the hospitality at the entrance and asking for the contact information should make it clear that this information will be used to send out the details of future events. Some people attending an event, especially for the first time, may not wish to give this information for a host of different reasons, but one fear may be that the church is going to send daily devotionals warning that if the visitor doesn't come for worship on the following Sunday morning, he or she is going to hell. The person may give a fake address or one created for junk mail. If someone looks hesitant about giving an e-mail or phone number, try asking for an address. People feel they can control what they open in the mail, as compared to e-mail or text messages. If the team finds that very few people are willing to give any form of information, then they may have a bigger problem. This resistance probably suggests that there is much fear and apprehension toward the church's intentions, and it will take several events for the unchurched to develop trust. If this happens, then the team may abandon their own need for the information so as to prioritize helping the unchurched feel that the church is trustworthy. Whatever is done with this information, the pastor cannot use it to show up at their doorstep, and the stewardship team should *absolutely* not use it to solicit a pledge.

A few days following the event, an e-mail or text should go out thanking people for their presence at the event and giving them the details about the next event. Some congregations may want to ask a few questions to help them plan for the next event, but they should do so cautiously. One congregation said, "We are trying to get to know our neighbors and want to make sure that the events we offer are of interest to them. Would you please take a few moments to answer the following three questions that will help us to plan future events?" Making a statement that answers the "why we are reaching out" question (to be addressed when we talk about framing invitations) may also serve to alleviate fears.

The Evaluative Phase

After an invitational event, the team that planned it will meet to do an evaluation. They may conduct their evaluation just prior to the meeting where the next team will begin planning the next few events. Overlapping the two teams gives the second team a chance to hear about the first team's perception of their successes and challenges so as to learn from their experience and design plans in light of these observations. Evaluating whether the event achieved the desired goal can save other teams from becoming frustrated and giving up. Teams that hold events and then do not take the time to evaluate tend to find that they repeat the same mistakes over and over again. Thus, the evaluative phase is one of the most important in planning invitational events.

The team will use the contact information to count how many unchurched people attended the event. This number will reflect how many members of the congregation invited someone. If, for instance, thirty unchurched persons attended an outdoor concert, the team can evaluate that the program to equip members to become invitational ministers has been successful for thirty members of the congregation. However, if a mass mailing was also used to invite the unchurched in the community, there may be no way of telling whether or not members actually personally invited friends and family. If it is evident that most of the people who attended the event were already members of the congregation, then the team may need to return to equipping the congregation to move from membership to discipleship by offering another workshop on invitational ministry. Determining the number of unchurched people who attend an event gives the team some numbers to evaluate how well the members are learning the skills for invitational ministry.

Numbers are important because—just as we count people who attend worship—when the number increases, it is an indicator that the behavior of individuals in the congregation is changing. This demonstrates that they are learning new skills and putting those skills into practice. When those who are sitting by the sidelines, trying to decide if they want to get in the game, witness that lives are changing and that people are excited about using these new skills to do the ministry that Jesus calls us to do, they are more likely to report for duty. Evaluating the event for its effectiveness by measuring how many disciples you are making among those who are churched, as well as among the unchurched, builds momentum and energizes a congregation to look at other new ways to spiritually form their faith.

Chapter 6

Framing Invitations

My parents were both raised in a Baptist church within the American Baptist denomination, and began dating while in youth group. When they got married and bought a home in a new neighborhood, a neighbor invited them to attend the Congregational church (United Church of Christ) down the street. My parents don't remember what this neighbor said in his invitation, but he conveyed that the church was a place where he and his family were learning about God and forming their faith. The church offered activities for families and an outstanding Christian education program for children. My parents were intrigued and visited the following Sunday. Later, they decided to join. I spent my childhood deeply committed to this church and its ministry. I don't know what my life would have been like if that neighbor had not invited my family to his church. I can witness to how one invitation can change people's lives.

This neighbor created incentive for my parents by witnessing to how his faith had been formed by the practices of the religious organization he attended. Back in the 1960s, that kind of an invitation would have been unusual, and is more in line with the kind of invitation that the unchurched are seeking today. In the 1960s, when a neighbor moved into the neighborhood and another neighbor of the same denomination learned of this connection, he or she simply knocked on the door and said, "I hear you are Methodist. My church is located down on Main Street. I hope to see you there on Sunday." The new neighbor may have been wondering where the nearest Methodist church was located and so the neighbor's invitation facilitated the process of finding a new church. The new neighbor would have been grateful that someone in the neighborhood took the initiative to help them locate points of interest around town.

In the twentieth century, when "everyone went to church," invitations were extended to people who were already churched. Factors such as location, times of worship, how long the pastor had been at that church, if the youth minister was paid, and the quality of the Christian education program all contributed to the decision to attend one church over another. Usually this choice was between two or three churches of the same denomination. Inviting someone who was churched by saying, "Would you like to try out our church? We love our pastor," was likely to garnish interest. Simply noting something that people were already looking for, such as a well-loved pastor, was enough. In other words, people knew what the church had to offer, and what they were specifically looking for. If they had young children, they were interested in Christian education. If they had youth, they were looking for a youth ministry program. If they had a history of being in a church with a pastor who was disliked, they were in search of a church with a beloved pastor, and so forth.

The ways of creating interest among the unchurched are different from those among the churched. Basically, the difference stems from the fact that the churched know what kinds of activities and programs a church has to offer, and, therefore, their search brings them to a place that offers what they are looking for. The unchurched know neither what they are looking for, nor what any particular church is likely to offer. They may sense that a religious organization offers alternative ways to form one's faith, but may also be unaware that these ways help one to spiritually connect with God in a manner significantly different from their own practices, done in the privacy of their home or lakeside retreat.

Why People Need an Invitation

I had an administrative assistant who used to tell the story about how she received a telephone call from a young woman who had recently moved her family into the neighborhood and was inquiring about a church to bring her children to attend. The reason for the telephone call was to ask whether or not she and her husband would need to take a test to determine how well versed they were in the Bible before they registered their children for Sunday school. The woman was obviously quite anxious about this and didn't want to come and then feel put "on the spot." My secretary assured her repeatedly that there was no test to register children for Sunday school, only a sign-up form that asked for contact information. She assured the woman that they would be warmly welcomed to attend worship that morning as well. We don't know if the woman ever brought her family to church, but it was a good reminder for the congregation that even among those who are interested in organized religion, there are questions about how to get in without an invitation.

Congregations who will be able to turn around their decline or to increase from a position of stability will be those who inspire and teach the members how to become invitational ministers. One way to inspire is to help members realize that there are people in the community who are hoping that they will be invited. It may turn out that while we are patiently waiting inside of the building hoping that a visitor will appear on the doorstop, the unchurched are patiently waiting at the doors of their homes, hoping that someone who is churched will show up to invite them. Let's not be too quick to assume that we need to create interest among the unchurched. Perhaps there are countless people in your own community right at this moment who are floundering in their faith, feeling empty inside, and searching for something meaningful.

There are other reasons why the unchurched need to be invited. As America becomes more ethnically and racially diverse, one important reason has to do with multiculturalism. If the unchurched are of a different ethnic group than most or all of the congregation, they need to be assured that they will be welcomed. A family from an ethnic group different from the congregation will visit one Sunday, and the first thing they will be thinking is, "Are there others like us here?" A church located in a racially and ethnically diverse neighborhood has to embrace diversity so they will then be able to practice invitation and hospitality with others from their own ethnic group. If they come and see no others, they are unlikely to return. For a congregation to become multicultural, a certain amount of intentionality about inviting friends and neighbors, with whom members personally have a relationship, goes a long way toward creating a hospitable environment that will allow those who are afraid of feeling marginalized to feel welcomed and respected.

When the congregations I served began numerically growing, we started asking the new members why they had not attended church previously. We wanted to better understand how to reach those who were unchurched. Repeatedly, we heard, "No one had ever invited me before." We asked if they had been curious or interested in the church and they said yes, but only if they could then cite something that the church was doing to make a difference in the community. Some lamented that they wished a member had invited them sooner, as they witnessed to personal crises and struggled to cope. They would say, "I wish I had had this community of faith at that time." We would also ask, "Would it have occurred to you to just show up on Sunday morning?" They frequently said, "No, I guess I didn't know that one could come without an invitation."

These statements reveal important insights. In my neighborhood growing up, I would walk into everyone's front door without knocking. The families all knew each other and we had a neighborhood culture that allowed children to freely walk in the front door of other children's homes. Back then, it would not have occurred to me to knock. But today, our culture honors a norm that says that you do not go on someone else's property without an invitation. I would not go to someone's home without calling first. When I am throwing the ball to my dog, and I accidently throw it too far into my neighbors' backyard, I knock on their door to get my neighbors' permission before retrieving it.

This current-day cultural norm is one reason that visitors are less likely to walk in the front door of our church buildings. They seem to think they need an invitation. Even if we don't think they should need one or think that they should *know* they don't need one, what is important to the process of making disciples is that we start meeting them where they are at. The congregation that says, "If they want to come, they know where to find us," has not yet realized that location is no longer the issue. I hear congregations talk about how, if the building were in a different location, they would be more visible to the community and increase their membership. Even a church located in the woods can be vital as long as its members are inviting others to attend.

Invitations for Those Interested in Church

The way we frame an invitation for those who are already interested in church, either because they were involved in a congregation before or have been involved recently but not actively, is much different from how we frame invitations that *create* interest. Those already interested may respond well to an invitation to attend church on a special Sunday. Please note: these invitations are meant to provide an entry point for them to either return or become more actively involved, not to create interest. Below are a few examples of an entry point invitation.

"Do you want to come with me to church?"

"I would be willing to pick you up and drive you to church on Sunday morning."

"Our church is having a Friendship Sunday, and, as my friend, I was hoping you would come."

"Our congregation has started a contemporary worship service if you would like to come."

"We have a new pastor who everybody likes. You should come and hear him preach."

"We are having a 'welcome back' Sunday for those who haven't been in church for a while and we're expecting quite a few people from the past. It should be a fun reunion and a chance to reconnect."

"This Sunday is rally Sunday. Are you interested?"

These invitations assume that the people being invited already have some interest in church because they know what the church has to offer. Entry points such as rally, welcome, friendship, and a new service provide an opportunity to attend. Invitations framed this way tend to work much more effectively among the dechurched who are waiting to be invited back but don't want to just show up one Sunday and be bombarded by other members asking, "Where have you been?" If they think that there will be other dechurched people present on a particular Sunday, it's easier to slide back into the swing of attending without being confronted.

Invitations for Those Not Interested in Church: Addressing Fears and Concerns

Not every unchurched person has interest in church and is waiting to be invited. In fact, probably the majority will need something more than an entry point invitation. Church members will need to create curiosity and interest within the frame of the invitation itself.

But before we begin talking about how to frame an invitation for those not interested in church, we need to examine some of their fears and concerns. It may be that they are not interested in church because they are opposed to organized religion. The unchurched tend to perceive that those who participate in organized religion are judgmental, hypocritical, and self-righteous, standing ready to denigrate those who are unchurched. They may fear that the reason they are being invited is to "brainwash" them to think the way churched people do. Given some episodes within the church's history, they may have good reason to be resistant to participating in church.

Invitational ministers need to be able to address these fears and concerns as they arise in conversations with the unchurched. Praying about these situations and how the present-day church can begin reconciliation and peace-building may inspire some church members, as well as those they are talking with, to become involved in social justice. Pretending these historical events did not happen, denying that the church played a role in enabling violence against the oppressed and persecuted, or enabling continued prejudice against the marginalized all contribute to a disdain among the unchurched for everything organized. By confessing our shortcomings, expressing our contrition, and talking about forgiveness, the churched and the unchurched can move forward together to right the wrongs that continue to plague our society and world.

Religion and Violence

Since the events of 9–11, many people have become increasingly sensitive to the connection between religious extremism and violence. The history of religious views justifying acts of violence is long. What might seem irrational to the wider public seems justified, even heroic, to those who feel violated.

Holocaust survivor and author Elie Wiesel brilliantly observes that we will never be able to end terrorism until we know what thoughts and feelings fueled such violent acts. Christians justified their own acts of violence during the Crusades. Those who opposed the abolitionist movement claimed that slavery was ordained by God. We ourselves are not exempt from supporting a religious institution that has not always taken the high road. Given our sins of actions and negligence, it's not surprising that religion is often perceived among young people to breed violence. What peace-loving person would want to be part of such an organization?

The disclosure of the sexual abuse of children by clergy, both Catholic and Protestant, has also contributed to the distrust of organized religion. Those who have historically been trusted are no longer viewed as trustworthy. In the eyes of many, that one ordained minister could sexually abuse a child translates into a mistrust of all ordained ministers. We have no way of knowing the ramifications that this trauma will have on the future of organized religion, but it is evident that it will have an impact.

Another major factor has been the intermingling of religion and politics. Given that the conservative voice generally has been louder than the liberal voice in the media recently, young people assume that the conservative agenda is the agenda of all religious organizations. Some unchurched young people are more tolerant and accepting of those from a wide range of multicultural groupings. They perceive that the church is passing judgment on their friends who are gay and lesbian, and they conclude, "I wouldn't want to have anything to do with an organization that rejects people I care about."

Religion and Multiculturalism

With respect to multiculturalism, many young people have had occasion to interact with persons of diverse ethnic and racial groupings. On college campuses as well as in corporate America, they are forming relationships with people from different ethnic backgrounds. When they enter a religious organization whose membership is comprised of one ethnic group, they wonder if this dynamic stems from segregation by choice, especially in neighborhoods that have become racially and ethnically diverse. Religious organizations are one of the last in society able to integrate people of diverse cultural backgrounds. The young are not interested in supporting segregation and can appreciate the benefits of multiculturalism given their experience. The churches that will survive this time of decline will be the ones that successfully transition from monocultural to multicultural.

Religion as Outdated

Young people also perceive that religious organizations are out of date—not just in terms of music or forms of worship, but in the images of God that the church preaches and teaches. In traditional congregations, God may be imaged as a white, elderly man with a long white beard, intertwined with the mythology of the Christmas figure. Those who describe themselves as spiritual but not religious may not imagine God as personal, with human characteristics, at all. They may understand God as a force, energy, or creative spirit. They often reject theology that says God punishes people who do bad things and the popular view that people go to church to learn how to do good. I often hear people speak from this viewpoint when they conclude, "I don't need to go to church because I am already a good person."

Religion Makes People "Super-Religious"

Some people imagine that church members sit around memorizing the Bible, chapter and verse, so that they can use scripture to justify their behavior and/or their point of view. They fear that the churched will use this knowledge in situations in which they (the unchurched) are sharing what they believe, so as to prove them "wrong." They are afraid of having such a conversation with someone who is churched because they expect that the churched person will try to convince them of the churched person's "rightness."

Religion and "Special Status"

The unchurched may also perceive that super-religious people will also behave aggressively as in-your-face evangelists on a mission to save them (the unchurched)—as if "heavenly points" were rewarded for accomplishing this task. They fear that the churched see themselves as among the "saved" and everyone else is going to hell. They may be afraid that the churched will look down on them, even pity them as the churched pronounce the unchurched doomed toeternal damnation. The unchurched may have had an evangelist knock on their door or confront them in public, condemning them. If so, they may (understandably) be hypersensitive to church people who seem to have an agenda. They fear they will be asked, "Aren't you afraid of going to hell?" When invited to an event, they need to be reassured that everyone is on the same journey, getting to know Jesus, and no one is better or more loved than anyone else. Assuring them that "we are all in this together" may address this fear.

The above concerns and fears may be on the minds of those who are unchurched within your congregation's neighborhood. Invitational ministers may discern other issues as well. I do not bring these issues up when making an invitation, but if the person being invited raises them, the invitational minister should respond to these concerns. Because we are among those who support organized religion, we are likely to want to defend it, but to do so will not likely change the minds of those who harbor these fears and concerns. Dismissing the concern by saying, "Oh, you have nothing to worry about in this church," also does not address these concerns directly. When possible, give specifics as to how your church takes these concerns seriously. For example, young families may be interested to learn that many churches have implemented "safe church policies" to protect their children from abuse. When an unchurched person expresses a concern, it's better to talk about what the church has done to confront this potential problem. One of the most powerful fears among the unchurched is that those who are churched have their heads in the sand and are oblivious. But many congregations today are being diligent about making their churches multicultural, contemporary, safe-for-children, peace-building places for all of God's children.

Fears/Concerns among Members: Helping Them to Feel More Comfortable Inviting

We invite people to join us in doing activities almost every day of our lives. We see an advertisement about a new movie that sounds interesting and we invite a friend to join us. We hear about a new restaurant opening in the neighborhood and we text a family member with an invitation to meet there for dinner. We notice a job opening posted at our workplace and we e-mail the information to a neighbor who is looking for employment. Every time we ask someone to join us for an activity, we are extending an invitation. Asking people to engage in an activity with us is something that we do with relative ease, without much intentional thought or anxiety.

So why do we cringe when we think about inviting people to church? Is there a difference between inviting people to join us for an activity and inviting them to church? If so, what is that difference? Are there skills we can develop to help us manage our anxiety and feel more confident about this new ministry? Do we believe that Jesus wants us to bring his church to another generation of believers (and bring them to the church)?

From the perspective of the unchurched, the difference between being asked to go to the movies and asked to go to church is that they've been to the movies. They know what to expect and what is expected from them. It's easier for people to decide to accept an invitation if they have been to the activity before and know whether or not it met a need. Many do not know what goes on in a church or during a worship service. They don't know what to expect or what is expected from them. Therefore, a simple invitation such as, "Do you want to come to church with me?" is likely to receive a negative response.

Those who are churched say they don't feel comfortable asking because they don't know what to say beyond a simple invitation. They have asked people to come to church, and over and over again people have said no. Eventually, they stop asking. Few people want to come across as pushy, so to preserve the relationship, they "know not to bring up the subject of church." But it is not necessarily the subject of church that the unchurched don't want to talk about. They may simply need something more than an invitation in order to make a decision. To complicate matters, they might not know what kind of information they do need. They are depending on the invitational minister to know how to frame an invitation in a way that peaks their curiosity.

Components of an Invitation

Simply asking persons to come to a religious organization and expecting that they will say yes, then, is not likely. In addition to fears and concerns about organized religion, invitational ministers will also need to create curiosity and interest among the unchurched. Curiosity can be spirited through the invitation itself. Invitational ministry is a conversation, and the invitational minister will need to learn what kinds of questions to ask to help persons who are unchurched discern their own interest in coming to an invitational event. Balancing curiosity and interest is a skill that invitational ministers can learn.

To invoke curiosity, I suggest that the frame of an invitation contain three components:

1. A witness to one's faith
2. A witness to how one's faith is formed through Christian practices associated with the church
3. A witness to the theological reason why the church is reaching out the unchurched

Component #1: Witnessing to One's Faith

Witnessing is essentially saying something about what one believes. The invitational minister does not need to go into depth, and this only has to be a sentence or two—perhaps something that is a core belief of one's faith.

Because faith-sharing may not have been an integral part of congregational life, leaders may need to plan exercises to help members to discern what they believe. Some may have never had an occasion to say out loud what they believe. It doesn't have to be framed in grand theological language. In fact, if it is too technical sounding or is something contained in a creed and memorized, it will not sound personal (and probably won't sound invitational either).

A witness can be a personal story of one's experience of God. It does not necessarily need to have happened within the context of the church, but it should be an experience that says, "This is my story." A witness does not seek to unravel the belief system of another. Sharing one's personal story is not a theological statement that is made so as to generate controversy or conflict. It is not meant to persuade (although it may be compelling and, therefore, persuasive). It is not framed as "what everyone else should believe." Your story may include statements that Christians believe, but should be open to counter-arguments. You are not trying to enter into a debate with someone who is unchurched. Let's consider the difference between traditional statements of faith and witnessing to one's faith.

Below are some examples of statements of faith.

"Jesus Christ is my Lord and Savior."

"Everything happens for a reason. God must have had a good reason for taking your loved one."

"I believe that God never gives us more than we can handle."

"Jesus Christ is the only way to heaven."

"God loves you."

"I don't think that science and religion are compatible."

Now, note the differences in the sentences below that witness to one's faith.

"When I was grieving the loss of my husband, I believe that God sent people from the church to help me find the strength to keep going."

"I just happened to show up at the right time to be able to help. I believe that it was the work of the Holy Spirit that brought me here."

"I believe that Jesus appears to us through other people. I met him once when I was building a house for Habitat for Humanity."

"I don't know why bad things happen to good people. What I do know is that God doesn't make those things happen. When I was going through a tragedy, I felt God continually by my side. I kept praying, "Please God, help me through this."

Component #2 Witnessing to How One's Faith Is Formed through Christian Practices

The second component of an invitation takes, "This is what I believe," to, "This is how I came to what I believe."

Among other reasons, people go to a religious service or event to experience God's presence. Most worship services are designed with this expectation. That's why we often begin with a prayer of invocation. Jesus says, whenever two or three are gathered in his name, he will be in the midst of them. Through that presence, as Christians we believe that we experience forgiveness, strength, caring, love. It's not so much the presence of God that we seek but what that presence does for us.

Here are some examples of witnessing to how one's faith is formed through Christian practice.

"I didn't think that God was there for me when I was in crisis, but in my small group at the church, others could see God doing things that I would never have realized, had I not had the opportunity to share my story."

"When I had cancer last year, I would go to worship on Sunday morning, and just knowing that everyone in the congregation was praying for me gave me the strength to handle whatever outcome lay ahead."

"I recently went through a divorce and I felt like I failed. By building relationships with my sisters and brothers in Jesus, I came to realize that I deserve to be loved by someone who appreciates me as a child of God."

"Before I started going to church, I felt something missing in my life. I didn't know what it was. Through participating in the programs in the church, I came to develop my spiritual life."

"I'm struggling with what I believe; I'm not even sure I believe in God. This church is a place to struggle with those issues. They don't tell you what you have to believe. They helped me to ask the questions."

"I believe in Jesus. He is my friend who walks with me and talks with me, just like the lyrics of the song. When I sing that song in worship, I know that no matter what lies ahead for me this week, I will be able to handle it."

"I don't attend worship in the church, preferring a small group of people to talk with about what is going on in my life. At first it was a little uncomfortable; I didn't know these people. Now, I feel like I can tell them anything and they won't judge me. They love me and support me, and I need that in my life right now."

"I attend the liturgical arts worship with a yoga mat. The pastor offers a guided meditation and they play sacred music. I also walk a labyrinth. It's different from doing yoga in a health club, because in the church, the time together is also a time of personal sharing."

Component #3: Witnessing to Why the Church Is Reaching out to the Unchurched

Each invitational minister will be saying something different as they share a personal story and connect that story to how their faith is formed through a Christian practice. The third component will be prayed about, formalized, and then memorized. Every invitational minister will be saying the same thing; almost word for word. Articulating the reason why this church is reaching out to this community is key to consistency—making sure that when

the unchurched begin talking with one another, they will confirm
that the church has a theological reason for reaching out, and not
a financial one. I suggest a few theological reasons below, but I
strongly encourage the congregation to discern its own. The
question to be answered is, "Why do you believe that God is calling
every member of your congregation to reach out to the
neighborhood and make disciples?"

Below I will share a few examples that congregations I have
worked with have discerned. These merely serve as illustrations
to give the reader some ideas.

"We believe that God calls us to share what we have with others."

*"Because going to this church is changing people's lives, we believe
that we say 'thanks to God' by inviting others to this experience."*

*"Our church woke up one day and we realized that we weren't doing
what Jesus wanted us to be doing; that is, inviting others to join us on the
journey."*

*"Our church wants to be more involved in the community. We think
we can make a difference but we realized that we can't do that if we walk
from the parking lot into the front door and then back to the parking lot
and drive home."*

*"Our congregation has been praying for the community. We are trying
to gather a group of concerned citizens to see what we can do together to
make a difference."*

To say nothing assumes that the church is reaching out for
self-serving reasons. I offer a few of those below to serve as
illustrations of what not to say.

*"The finance committee just gave a report and we realize that if we
don't do something, we're not going to be around next year."*

*"We're doing a membership drive and I am wondering if you would
be willing to join the church."*

*"I raised you in the church—the least you could do for me is to bring
my grandchildren. If you aren't willing to come, then can I pick them up
and bring them?"*

*"We believe that God wants our church to be around for another
generation so we are hoping to attract some young people in our
neighborhood to come to church."*

*"People in this community are going to realize that when our church
has to close, it won't be there any longer to help them. Then, they'll be sorry."*

"We have chosen to do a turnaround, so that means that we need to numerically grow our congregation."

Designing Workshops for Members

I suggest that the team design a series of three workshops to equip members with the skills for invitational ministry. Each workshop is planned with tasks to teach disciples to invite people who are unchurched. Below, I will outline suggestions for agenda-setting that will help with this process. Initially, the pastor will probably need to take the lead in teaching these skills. The pyramid method of equipping is for the pastor to learn the skills and teach a few key leaders in the congregation skilled at teaching, who then teach others. What begins with one trained leader (the pastor) then continues to stretch to include many others.

At the beginning of this process, leaders may feel overwhelmed at times and will need to depend on other members for assistance. The objective is to get as many people as possible involved in the process. A pastor who continues to need to control this process by doing all the teaching and/or stand as the crucial center with everyone else spinning around, will undermine getting others involved. I also suggest that if a nearby congregation is further along in the process of equipping invitational ministers, a few of its members could to do the training in the workshops or help out.

Some will say, "I am too old," to which we respond, "One is never too old to do the work of Jesus." Some will say, "I am too shy," to which we respond, "Shyness can be an asset because then people know how difficult it is for you to be able to do this." Excuses will be free-floating and forthcoming. The goal is to get 100 percent participation. Those who helped to make the decision to do a turnaround signed up for these workshops when they made that decision. If they adopted the "whatever it takes" attitude, then the pastor reminds them, "This is what it takes." If the majority of members do not attend the workshops, the pastor will need to help them to revisit this decision.

These workshops are designed with two objectives in mind. One, most members say that the primary reason they don't invite others is because they don't know what to say. If they do not know what to say, then these workshops will teach them how to go about framing an invitation. The second objective is to reduce (not alleviate) their anxiety so they feel confident and willing to extend an invitation. The first objective will help with the second objective: when members know what to say, they will feel more confident. Building confidence is good for the emotional health of the individual. It is also good for invitational ministry: those who are invited by someone who appears confident are more likely to accept an invitation.

Children and youth should also be taught to be invitational ministers. A workshop should address the unique way that they will go about inviting their friends. To assure they will invite others in a way that ensures their safety, those who are well trained to communicate with children and youth should be the ones who give instructions. Children and youth don't seem to have inherited the collective anxiety about inviting their friends, and so often already do so with ease. They should not be taught to invite those whom they do not know because that may send a mixed message when their parents have taught them not to talk with strangers. A workshop for children and youth might also address the reasons for inviting others, so that they understand the theology behind this effort.

When a child or youth does invite a friend to attend an event or worship service, I suggest that their parents follow-up with a contact to the parent or parents of the person they have invited. This conveys that the congregation is practicing safe-church policies. In the past, we used to hope that a young person would come to youth group and their parents would follow behind by showing up for worship. Today, many parents would not be comfortable allowing their children to attend a church activity if they are not familiar with the church and/or people in the congregation. Taking the initiative to speak with a parent whose child is interested in attending an event demonstrates that the congregation is open to a conversation about the child's safety, as well as any concerns that the parent or parents may have. This may even be an opportunity to invite the parents also.

Workshop #1: Motivation for Inviting (Personally and Collectively)

There are reasons why a congregation finds itself in decline. Some stem from outside factors such as cultural shifts, norms, and expectations. Others arise from within the organization and are enabled by the current membership. The reasons why members have denied or allowed the decline for some time should be identified, articulated, and confessed. Members aren't inviting others. Sometimes, they don't necessarily want more members and/or change, and new people come with new ideas. Some may have resisted the efforts of others because they were afraid of losing their power and status within the congregation. Be it apathy, indifference, or outright resistance to numerical church growth, each member has not done his or her part to make disciples of the unchurched in the neighborhood.

During the devotional to begin this workshop, worship leaders should design a ritual of confession. Members need to confess their shortcomings to God and know the forgiveness that comes to us through Jesus. In most circumstances, members are well aware that the pastor has preached about helping others beyond the congregation, and they have not done so. This is an opportunity to correct that behavior and to honor Jesus' commission to do his work as his disciples. Guilt tends to immobilize people, and so a ritual that helps people to redirect their guilt with the experience of forgiveness (rather than let go of it and let themselves off the hook) motivates them for this ministry. A ritual may ask members to write down on a piece of paper why they have not been inviting others, and then ask them to bring forward their paper and place it in a tin on the altar. The leaders then burn the papers and place the ashes on members' foreheads to commission them for invitational ministry.

The first workshop addresses the motivational factors for invitational ministry. Members may need an opportunity to voice why they are not inviting (the same things they wrote down on the pieces of paper) as well as their own fears and concerns. Leaders will consider two aspects of motivation: why the congregation as a collective wants to engage in invitational ministry and the personal positives that will improve the life of the individual by doing so. One way to collectively motivate a congregation is for them to better know their neighbors. Speaking of the unchurched as a collection of amorphous people "out there" doesn't do much to inspire members. Conveying that these are real people with real needs who experience the same kind of feelings and struggle with the same theological issues as those inside the church goes a long way toward dispelling members' concerns and redirecting them to address the needs of the unchurched.

Those who did the prayer walks in the neighborhood and the Internet searches on the computer can report their findings at this point. Pictures of community events may be projected onto a screen. Use photos of people around town, landscapes, and buildings to illustrate the team's assessment about whether the neighborhood is "up and coming" or "been there and declining." This addresses the "why now?" issue. If the neighborhood is up and coming, the congregation has a window of opportunity to reach out to those who are moving into the neighborhood. If the neighborhood is declining, members will know to focus on meeting the social service needs of the neighborhood and/or offering something unique that motivates people to commute in. Demographics should show who is out there, and can be presented in either graph or chart form.

Knowing the neighborhood so that we can love our neighbor sets the stage for introducing component #3, "Why are we reaching out to our neighborhood?" The first workshop will only introduce this question, because it will require time for members to pray about it as individuals and then collectively during worship. The answer will be a collective one that everyone believes is the reason God has placed this church in this neighborhood. Leaders might suggest that members keep a journal of their own prayers and meditations on this question so that, in the second workshop, members can have a discussion about what God has revealed to them. Hopefully, they will build consensus around the answer (without voting).

Most congregations will embark on this journey to become invitational ministers, though their collective reason for becoming invitational ministers may still be money and more members, and this hovers just over the surface of every conversation. Leaders may need to continually emphasize that the mission is not to fill the pews with more bodies but to offer spiritual formation to those who are unchurched. Numerical church growth is one indicator that invitational ministers are making disciples of others. The organization exists for the purpose of forming people's faith and offers Christian practices that assist in this process. Therefore, a theological reason for practicing invitational ministry keeps members focused on why the church is doing this. Congregations that focus on organizational needs will struggle with motivating individuals to reach beyond their comfort level and change their behavior.

Leaders will also want to help members to identify what I refer to as "the personal positives" for practicing invitational ministry. These may include, but are not limited to, psychological reasons such as raising self-esteem, building self-confidence, and feeling competent with learning new skills and practicing them, as well as spiritual reasons such as feeling more connected to God, sensing the Holy Spirit working through them, and becoming more aware of the teachings of Jesus. Doing the work of the Trinity is itself life transforming, and you need to equip members to experience this for themselves. Hopefully, the pastor will know how this works and be able to witness to how he or she has experienced his or her own personal positives.

Workshop #2: Framing the Invitation (Content)

In the second workshop, members will meet in small groups to discern a story that reveals their faith (component #1) and how that faith was formed through a Christian practice (component #2). This workshop seeks to answer the question, "How does the organization help me to form my faith?" It is not enough to simply witness to faith. An effective invitation also witnesses to how the organization facilitates this process. A church that is not designed to be part of this process or functions contrary to this process (by overextending people to do management tasks rather than ministry) should not invite others. If the church has nothing to offer, the unchurched might as well continue to worship God in their backyard (a lot less busy work!). The first exercise helps members to talk about their faith, and the second exercise connects the formation of their faith with the church. Worship, Bible study, support groups, adult education, social justice projects, and so forth are all ways to form faith. Leaders may identify a variety of Christian practices.[1]

The second workshop also revisits the question, "Why is the congregation reaching out to the community?" Now, it is time to build consensus around the answer. The point of consensus is so that every member is in the community saying the same thing. I suggest that members memorize a script that they will repeat every time someone in the community asks them this question. Without this consensus, members might be saying different things to their neighbors, and, when their neighbors inevitably begin comparing notes, they may realize that they have received mixed messages. For instance, if one member says, "We are reaching out to get to know our neighbors and their needs," and another member says, "We are reaching out because we need the money," the neighborhood will not perceive that the church is being honest and transparent about its motivation. A church that encourages anything that may be perceived as dishonesty only feeds the commonly held perception by the unchurched that the church is filled with hypocrites.

Workshop #3: Practicing Becoming Invitational Ministers

The focus of the third workshop is to give members an opportunity to learn and practice skills for invitational ministry. In between the second and third workshop, all the invitational ministers will have discerned their stories of how the church helped them to form their faith. They are feeling more confident now that they know what to say, framing an invitation in a way that is more likely to get a positive response. They have their invitations framed with the three components and they have prayed about how they will respond to the fears and concerns that the unchurched might address with them. They are now ready to practice.

Before invitational ministers begin inviting each other to church, I suggest they begin with a different exercise. Leaders will ask everyone, "What organization or type of organization are you the least likely to have any interest in attending?" They can then list these on a white board, flip chart, or screen so members can refer to them. Then divide the group into pairs and ask each invitational minister to invite the other to one of these organizations. This exercise helps them to develop empathy for those they will be inviting. "What would I need to hear to be curious about attending an organization that, at this moment, I have little (if any) interest in attending?" Members tend to enjoy this exercise and have fun with it. Leaders might then ask, "Did anyone succeed in getting their partner to say yes to attending?" Hopefully, members will have a new perspective for what it is like to be invited to an organization that they wouldn't consider attending without an invitation.

Also during this workshop, leaders may suggest a few questions that can serve to lead a conversation with the unchurched toward a talk to discern their spiritual needs and interests. The following are some suggestions.

"It sounds like you are wrestling with similar concerns. I'm wondering if you have given some thought about how the church might help you to explore your options."

"When you say you are 'spiritual but not religious,' what does that mean to you?"

"I sense that your experience of God in nature has been valuable to the formation of your faith. Have you considered attending an outdoor worship service? Our church holds one over the summer."

"Have you found it helpful in the past to talk about your experiences of God?"

The invitational minister should not identify, "This is what I think you would gain from attending our church." The point of witnessing is to help the unchurched identify with the story so that they make their own connections. While an invitational minister is sharing his or her witness, hopefully, the unchurched listener is thinking, "I wonder if going to a Bible study at that church would make me more able to open up to my spouse?" or, "I haven't thought about God for a long time. I wonder if it's time for me to get reconnected?" When we say things such as, "This is what I think you need," we tend to guess wrong, or others feel judged. Invitational ministers plant seeds of interest. It is up to those being invited to decide that attending a religious organization might be helpful to their spiritual growth.

The third workshop also provides an opportunity to practice inviting others to church. Role playing by using one's framed invitation allows for immediate feedback. In a learning environment, members should trust one another enough to give an honest response so that the invitational minister can refine the invitation if need be. Responses such as, "When you told me that story, it really made me curious about how you had figured that out," or, "It made me feel awkward when you started talking about that situation," help invitational ministers test out their invitations. They might follow up with a question such as, "If I said it this way, do you think it would sound different?" Asking for feedback allows them to reframe their invitations if necessary. Members will have an emotional investment in working cooperatively to ensure that everyone will be offering invitations that hold the most promise for making disciples.

An invitation that is well framed and creates interest should be affirmed. The exercise should be designed so that each invitation, when formed from the heart, is transforming the one who is becoming a disciple. Members who hear positive feedback and feel good about their newly acquired skills now feel equipped for this new ministry. For too long the church has empowered people for ministry but not equipped them with the skills that they need. Only after these three workshops should leaders empower members "to make disciples of all nations." They are now ready. It is time to send them out into the neighborhood to begin inviting their friends and family members, colleagues and neighbors to attend invitational events.

Chapter 7

Avenues to Extend Invitations

Recently, I consulted with a church and asked all the members, one at a time, to introduce themselves and tell me how they arrived at this particular church. Responses ranged from, "I was born into this church," to, "I moved into the neighborhood and came to this church because it was the denomination I had been raised in." Twenty-six people shared how they became members. When they had each responded, I observed that not one person had come this church through an avenue of invitation. The historical means by which people formerly came to a church are not the ways the unchurched find their way into the church. Today, the most likely reason persons who are unchurched attend worship service is because someone invited them. How many more people are likely to come if we offer invitational events as another entry point into the life of a congregation?

As the congregation I served began to realize that we needed to look at the different avenues available to us to extend an invitation to people in our neighborhood, it became important for me to model what I was asking members of the congregation to do.

In the midst of a worship service, I asked everyone to stand who had met me while we were both running or walking on a treadmill and started up a conversation. About twelve people slowly rose and waved to the congregation. After the first series of invitational events, I asked everyone to stand who had come to the worship service because a member of the congregation had invited them to one or several of the invitational events. Quite a few people stood up, to the awe of the congregation. We were not only learning how to invite others, we were learning where to go to have a conversation with others that could lead to being able to invite them to an event.

This chapter explores the where and how to extend an invitation. I will suggest several places that are most conducive to talking with people we do not know. While initially most members will begin using their invitational ministry skills to invite friends and family members, they will also need to venture out to get to know their church's neighbors through prayer walks and Internet searches.

Two Basic Forms of Invitations

Invitations take two forms: personal and mass. A personal invitation is extended from one person to another. A mass invitation can be a mailing sent through the post office to addresses in the neighborhood, a sign out front of the church, or a brochure handed out by members of the congregation in front of a supermarket. Both forms of invitation can be effective in reaching the unchurched, depending on the nature of the event, the culture of the neighborhood, and how many other congregations are using this same form of invitation. A personal invitation is given to people we already have a relationship with (friends, colleagues, neighbors) as well as people we meet through interest groups–from quilting guilds to fantasy football league–or those with whom we strike up a conversation in the grocery store check-out line. The recipients of a mass invitation are usually people we don't know and are unlikely to come into contact with to allow us to issue a personal invitation.

Overall, personal invitations tend to be more effective than mass invitations. One reason is because they give two people an opportunity to have a conversation about coming to church. The unchurched person can voice concerns, express fears, and ask questions in response to being invited. In many respects, an invitation is not so much an invitation to an event as it is an invitation to a conversation about church in general. The personal nature of this kind of invitation also allows for the beginning of a new relationship or the nurturing of a long-term one by having a discussion about something that perhaps has not been discussed previously, such as faith, church, or spirituality. An invitational minister now possesses the skills to address fears and concerns about religious organizations and discern the interests of the unchurched. A mass invitation cannot accomplish any of these things.

The church growth strategies of the 1980s and 1990s used mass invitations in bulk with the hope of stirring the interests of the neighborhood. These invitations focused almost exclusively on getting people to come to worship. Some churches sent out thousands of postcards (and every once in a while I still get on in the mail) inviting their neighbors. Once a few churches started doing this, every other church followed suit. Most congregations that did try this avenue of invitation reported a low rate of return on a costly venture. I understand that if we change one life, it may be worth sending out thousands of invitation postcards, but, for the most part, mass invitations are less effective than personal invitations.

Mass invitations should not be used as a substitute for personal invitations, but in combination with them. When a neighbor receives a mass invitation for an event and then a few days later meets someone from the church who extends a personal invitation, this lends credence to the invitation itself. He or she is likely to respond with, "Oh, I think I received something about that in the mail. Yes, I was thinking about going. I need some details, though." This is especially true when we talk about canvassing from door to door. The postcards sent out beforehand legitimate the person showing up at one's doorstep. The postcards might even be designed to state that "someone from our congregation will be coming through the neighborhood next Saturday."

The point is that mass invitations should not be the invitation of choice because they relieve invitational ministers from feeling uncomfortable talking with friends, family, and neighbors. A congregation should not expect that sending out a mass mailing will be the answer to decline or that people will begin showing up in droves for Sunday morning worship. That is not going to happen. Numerical growth happens because a congregation gets to know its neighbors and their interests and needs, and personally invites them to attend events. There is no substitute for a personal invitation. So we begin by equipping invitational ministers to extend personal invitations.

Personal Invitations (also see chapter 6 on framing invitations)

Unless I know for sure that someone is churched and have heard him or her recently speak about involvement, I assume that everyone I know and everyone I meet is unchurched. This is a safe assumption, given the latest statistics, on the number of unchurched in North America. They vary widely in neighborhoods across the country, ranging from 20 to 80 percent An even more sobering thought is that, whatever the percentage of unchurched in your neighborhood, it is likely increasing. In addition, more and more people are exiting church life, burned out from so many tasks needing to be done by so few people, and because many of our mainline members are retiring and not rejoining another church.

Assuming that everyone I know and everyone I meet is unchurched or dechurched affords me the opportunity to have a conversation with anyone about church. If people are churched, they will tell me about their church, and the joys and struggles of congregational life. Members like to talk about their pastor and what is currently going on in their church. No matter what is going on in the life of the church, most members find something positive to say about their involvement and like being asked. Asking, "How are things going in your church?" is equivalent to asking, "How are things going for you?" for a generation whose identity is intimately tied to belonging to a religious organization.

When I am talking with someone at the gym about church and discover that they are not churched, I have a few topic starters that help get the conversation going. For instance, I might ask, "Have you ever been to a church?" "What was that experience like for you?" "Do you know anyone who goes to church?" "Have you ever wondered what people do in there on Sunday morning?" "Has anyone ever invited you to church ?" "What kinds of spiritual programs might interest you?" "Do you go to yoga class here at the gym? If it were offered would you go to yoga class in a church?"

Church members tend to assume that everyone they know and everyone with whom they come into contact on a daily basis is already churched (just as it was in the 1960s). They are often surprised to learn that some of their friends who had previously been active in a church haven't been there for years. Members who become inactive often find it difficult to reveal their inactivity to their friends because of the generational norm that says, "Everyone goes to church somewhere." They may feel guilt about their lack of involvement and so would not bring it up on their own. When a friend begins the conversation, they may be relieved to be able to talk about why they stopped attending church and what would need to change for them to feel comfortable returning. The conversation itself may change someone's life as they prayerfully contemplate returning to their home congregation. If that is not an option for them, then the invitational minister may invite them to attend his or her church.

A member told me how every week his friend would ask him to play golf on Sunday morning. Every time his friend asked, he would say, "Now you know I go to church every Sunday morning." This went on for some time, until finally the member said, "Why do you keep asking me to play golf on Sunday morning when you already know that I go to church?" and his friend replied, "I kept hoping that you would invite me to come with you to church."

By asking friends about their church involvement, we might also find that they only attend periodically or around the holidays. They may feel obligated to attend worship at certain times of the year, but they do not participate in the life of the congregation. Something may be blocking them from participating in that particular church. If they have an emotional tie to this church because, for instance, it was the church of their childhood, they may continue to attend during the holidays. Talking about their involvement may be a way to help them to think about what it would be like to be active in that church or another. The invitational minister might ask questions about whether they feel they are getting what they need from church by attending infrequently, or if they may be interested in attending a church where they could become more involved. Sometimes just having this conversation with your friends can be life changing for them.

Places Where People Are Likely to Hang out and Be Receptive to Conversation

Throughout most of history, people gathered at churches to worship God, meet new people, and catch up on the local news.

At this moment in history, those days seem to be gone. These days, people are more likely to gather in coffee shops and health clubs. They meet new people and talk about the concerns of the community, and may even have a conversation about faith. In both coffee shops and health clubs, people seem more at ease talking with people they do not know. The same people may frequent these settings at the same time of day and may begin to recognize other people who do likewise. This recognition seems to give permission for conversation, i.e., "I see you in here each week." Members will need to survey their neighborhoods to discover these places where people hang around so that they can begin feeling comfortable having a conversation with those who are unchurched– a conversation that may lead to inviting them to an event.

Coffee shops and cafes are great places to meet new people, especially the unchurched. In the Penn Central Conference of the United Church of Christ, we are equipping pastors and leaders to hold book studies in coffee shops. A pastor or leader invites three other people from the congregation to join in offering a weekly book study that meets in the same location for up to twelve weeks. Each week the group sits in the same chairs with plenty of extra books in the middle of the table. They engage others who happen to be in the coffee shop at the same time; if someone at a nearby table overhears the conversation and chimes in, there is an extra book to use so that he or she can join the conversation. (I recommend that the group give the book to the person free of charge. Sometimes, this will help people to feel obligated to return the following week.) The book should address religious questions, such as, What is the meaning of life? What happens after we die? Why do bad things happen to good people?

Each of the participants from the congregation may invite an unchurched friend to attend, and the group may hang up a sign in the coffee shop inviting others. The sign should include the purpose of the group and meeting time details. Check with the owner of the coffee shop before hanging a sign. (The owner of one coffee shop joined the book study group!) Make it clear that this is a book study from the local church and again, when participants ask why the church is doing a book study out in the local coffee shop, have a theological reason to articulate (and this should be the same reason the invitational ministers are using in the community). When the group grows to about twelve participants (or smaller, depending on the size of the coffee shop), the congregation needs to begin a new group with four other members from the congregation. A group with more than twelve means that some people will not get a chance to speak. The group of four may find that they need to exercise patience and continue to meet each week until the group starts growing. Most book groups have a shelf life, so after twelve weeks they can either choose to read another book and continue to meet in the coffee shop, or a member of the congregation(not the pastor) can invite the nonmembers to attend an invitational event at the church or to worship.

The success of these groups depends on a couple of factors. One, the time and day that the group chooses to meet should not be random or chosen because it is convenient for the three members and the pastor or leader. The time should be selected based on the church's mission field. If the congregation is hoping to attract retired people to the church (not an easy demographic to engage), then a morning book study over coffee may be the best time. If the mission field is young families, then the morning is probably not a good time. Some groups have reported to me that in a community where young professionals are working, a book study over lunch (with food) has worked well for them, especially in neighborhoods that are filled with people during the day who do not live there. This may be a way to overcome not having enough young families in the neighborhood from which to draw new members. Those who form relationships with members might be willing to commute in.

A second factor determining success was whether the groups used personal and/or mass invitations. Some groups used personal invitations and members invited friends and family members. Other groups used mass invitations, hanging up signs in the coffee shops to invite those whom they did not know. Still other groups used both personal invitations and a sign in the coffee shop. The groups that used both personal and mass invitation reported the most participation by others (beyond the original four). The problem with only issuing personal invitations is that people in the coffee shop didn't know that they could join the group. The problem with only hanging up signs (and most of the groups that only hung signs didn't get anyone to join them and found the whole project frustrating) is that when others observe the same four people week after week, they may wonder why others are not joining the group, even if they might be interested. The groups that invited people they knew and people they did not yet know also reported that they had success in bringing in new people into the life of the congregation.

Mass Invitations

Mass invitations come in all shapes and sizes. Postcards, brochures, and newspaper inserts can all be effective (but the use of a lot of paper may not be in the best interests of a congregation trying to go green and appeal to the young generation). Mass invitations that invite to events tend to have a better response than those inviting to a worship service.

Another popular mass invitation is a church sign. Some signs have been in front of a church for so many years, saying nearly the same thing ("All Are Welcome"), that, at this point, they blend into the landscape and people no longer even make note of them. A church sign that "welcomes all' is not really an invitation. One might wonder if that is open to discussion. Signs that post sermon titles may be effective if the sermon title is intriguing and creative. A new trend employs electronic signs that light up or use blinking lights. They are designed to get people's attention, but I fear they reek of desperation. The more a church has to go to extremes, the more the neighborhood will wonder what is going on inside the organization that they are resorting to electronic signs.

A sign announcing an invitational event may be effective, depending on the nature of the event. A sign should never read "free to the public" because the public is thinking that they would rather pay upfront than have something else expected from them like being pushed into joining the church. The risk of not stating that the event is free is that some people will wonder what it costs and whether it is a fund-raiser for the church. They will not expect a "let's get to know our neighbors" event. Fund-raisers also tend to signal the community that the church is experiencing financial problems and therefore may be looking for new members.

Signs may be more effective when the congregation is inviting others to participate in a social justice project. People are looking for ways to make a difference within their community. An invitation to be involved in promoting environmental awareness or the impact of global warming may attract a number of young people in an urban area. If a family in a rural area has lost their barn to a fire, the church could coordinate a community-wide effort to help rebuild it. If there is a current topic that everyone in the community is talking about, booking a speaker with expertise on that topic shows the community that the congregation is aware of community concerns. Mass invitations that encourage people to be involved in their community signals to the community that the church cares about them.

Other Avenues of Invitation

Social Justice Projects

Like the churched, the unchurched have a spiritual need to make a difference in their community.

This avenue is perhaps the most likely to engage young people into the life of a congregation, but that engagement depends on how they are invited, what kind of project the congregation will be working on (whether or not they feel passionate about it) and who will be involved in the project. Personal invitations work well, such as, "Would you be willing to donate a few Saturdays to helping our church build a house in the community for Habitat for Humanity?" Most people will say "yes" (and they don't need to have carpentry skills!). Interestingly, I have found that mass invitations also work well. A sign in front of the church inviting people in the community to gather at the church to engage in a social justice project will likely get people in the neighborhood to participate.

Social justice projects such as environmental causes—helping buildings and homes in the area go green, organic gardens that feed those who are struggling financially, or helping other churches to use resources to put solar panels on their roofs—are likely to interest people in the neighborhood. Other projects that address equal rights issues such as marriage equality (passing the law that the gay and lesbian community has the right to be legally married) or economic equality (for example, the Occupy Movement) are controversial but will bring in young people who care about these issues. There are also area-specific issues that the neighborhood itself is struggling to build consensus around (for example, whether to continue to have a football team that has a politically incorrect name). The church can hold a forum so that both sides of the issue can come together and understand each other's interests.

Congregations should also be engaged in projects such as feeding the hungry through community meals, soup kitchens, or food pantries; or recycling clothing by offering a thrift shop. If the church is not located in a neighborhood that needs such social services, it should consider teaming up with another church in a neighborhood in need. These ministries show that members care about their neighbors.

This is *not* to say that meeting the social service needs of your community is a way to grow a church numerically. Those who are recipients of food, recycled clothing, or another service are not likely to attend an invitational event or worship. They are not in a line for a soup kitchen because they want to build relationships with people from the congregation (at least that is not their primary objective). They are hungry and need to be fed. I have heard members say, "We used to offer a soup kitchen but no one ever came back on Sunday morning." We feed the hungry and cloth the naked because Jesus calls us to do this ministry, not because we are hoping to turn the needy into members. We can and should invite them to invitational events and/or worship, but that should not be the primary reason why we are engaged in this ministry. Jesus calls us to feed the hungry and clothe the naked, , in so doing, we may be doing it for him (Mt. 25:31–46).

Congregations who feel that God is calling them to offer a community meal for those who are hungry or lonely or who enjoy eating with other people will realize that this is a great way to connect with the neighborhood. The meal provides opportunities for conversation, depending on whether they are serving the meal or sitting side by side eating. Too often, those who are offering the meal stand in the kitchen doing the dishes talking with one another, while those receiving the meal sit at the tables talking with one another. The planners of the meal should create opportunities for both groups to talk and interact with each other. Those who are serving the meal might ask some of those who show up for the meal to help serve while those who cooked the meal sit down and eat with the other guests.

Congregations (or outreach teams) that offer a community meal tend to be the ones who do it all: they purchase, prepare, and serve the food. In some situations, members perceive that "If I don't do it, no one else will." That may be indeed the case, but doing it oneself may be a missed opportunity to get other people involved. Too often, the perception is that no one else will help with a project, but, in reality, no one else has been asked. People want to be asked to participate in a worthwhile project, yet they often feel that they are treading on someone else's territory, especially if the same people have been doing the project for many years. Few people will volunteer when a pastor asks from the pulpit for people to do so. These kinds of social justice projects are a great way to get the unchurched involved in a congregation. Members should be inviting their friends and family to help serve rather than doing it themselves. Ideally, an outreach team becomes the coordinator of outreach, as opposed to in the committee model, in which the members on the committee tend to be the ones who do the outreach themselves.

I saw a young couple getting out of their car while I was coming out of the church one day. I approached them, introduced myself, and told them that I was looking for a couple to serve at the community meal next Saturday for two hours. I assured them that there would be some people to show them what to do. "Would you be willing to help out with this?" I asked, and they agreed and committed to being there. I then asked, "Do you have a couple of friends whom you would like to also invite to help out?" They looked at each other and began talking about whom they would invite. My reasoning in asking them to invite others is that they would probably feel more comfortable if they were coming with people with whom they already had a relationship, and the four of them together were likely to honor this commitment. (One person can say, "Oh, if I don't show up that won't make much difference.) The next week, I might ask the four if they have other friends that they would like to invite, until this new group is now "on" for that particular Saturday.

Canvassing

Canvassing is another avenue of invitation worth prayerfully considering. An advantage is that it is both personal (people from the congregation invite the person at the door to an event) as well as a mass invitation because they can knock on many doors and cover a wide range in an afternoon.

Unfortunately, canvassing has a shady reputation. Many members are uncomfortable with the idea of knocking on people's doors, primarily because they have had people come to their door saying things like, "Aren't you afraid of going to hell?" Similarly, those in the neighborhood dread opening their doors to encounter someone whose own eternal destiny depends on the conversion of others. Plus, we all know stories of people opening the door for robbers and becoming victims of violent crimes. Most of us hear our mothers' words of caution: "Don't open the door for anyone you don't know." Some neighborhoods have a culture that frowns upon knocking on someone else's door, but where I live in Harrisburg, people frequently come to the door asking me to sign a petition, inviting me to church, or making me aware of recent crime.

Canvassing can be effective under certain conditions. One, the canvassers should match the demographics of the neighborhood. If the congregation is trying to attract young families to an event, and they have decided to go around the neighborhood knocking on doors and handing out brochures inviting people to a concert, the canvassers should be young people. If the event is geared toward retirement-age people and the neighborhood is becoming increasingly comprised of people retiring, someone who is of retirement age should do the canvassing. Because so many mainline congregations are aging, some have tried sending out elderly members to neighborhoods with young families moving in, only to find out that no one new came to church the following Sunday.

Most congregations attract people like themselves. Multicultural congregations make an effort to widen this spectrum through intentional practices that bring more diversity. Many numerically large congregations have grown on the principle that "like" people attract other "like" people. We can apply this principle to canvassing (young canvassers will attract other young canvassers), but we should also not limit ourselves. We should simply realize that this is a natural tendency and work with it rather than try to work against it. If a congregation has been able to attract a few families from another ethnic background, one of these couples will be ideal as canvassers if the mission field reflects their ethnicity.

For safety reasons, I also recommend that canvassers go out in teams of two or three. They may wear t-shirts with the picture of the church so as to inspire confidence and trust. I also warn, "Never ever go into someone's home who you do not know." I recommend that the canvassers stay a few feet away from the door and prepare themselves for whoever may be answering the knock. If invited into the home, canvassers should say, "We are not allowed to enter people's homes, but thanks for inviting us!" and walk away.

What Should Canvassers Say?

I recommend that canvassers keep it short and sweet. They should introduce themselves with their first names and then go right into the invitation to the event. "Hi, we are Emily and Joshua and we attend the Presbyterian Church. We are having a concert next week for all the young families in our neighborhood. We hope to see you there!" In some situations, it may be appropriate to invite people to church, especially if they are new to the neighborhood. "Hi, we are Kyle and Bethany, and we live in that house over there. We are just going around the neighborhood introducing ourselves. We attend the church down the street (point in the direction), and if you don't have a church home, we hope you will join us some time."

If the canvassers are hearing a good response, "Yes, we will be there. Thanks for inviting us. It's next Saturday at 4:00? Sounds good," they may consider using that to create interest among others in the neighborhood by also saying, "It sounds like quite a few of your neighbors are planning on coming, and we hope you come to!" People are often afraid that they are going to be the only visitors at a church and will be pounced upon to join. Making them aware that there will be many visitors at this event and that it is going to be popular in the neighborhood may increase their willingness to attend. In a neighborhood with many young people moving in, the congregation not only needs to plan an event that is especially designed to appeal to this age range, but needs to make sure that they have extended enough personal invitations to assure that there will be other young families in attendance for the event.

The Internet

The Internet has become one of our contemporary avenues for invitation. It is also probably one of the most underutilized by religious organizations. In time, this will change. Using the Internet to communicate and invite will not only appeal to the young generation but all those who are concerned about the environment. For instance, congregations that are still sending out paper newsletters or paper (printed) invitations may be "advertising" that they are functioning in an outdated mode.

Facebook

Facebook is one of the most frequented websites on the Internet. Organizations can list themselves and their events and then ask their friends to "like" the organization. In the process of inviting a large group of people to an event, invitational ministers can invite their friends to the event on Facebook. This is easy to do at the click of a button. The unchurched are not likely to search out the church's page, but they will see the activity if everyone is "liking" the event and inviting others. Inviting the unchurched through Facebook is more of a personal invitation than a mass invitation. A generation who has not grown up using Facebook may see it as a mass invitation, but the current generation who frequents Facebook will consider it a personal invitation.

Websites

Most congregations today have websites. This avenue of invitation first requires interest within the organization. Acting as a personal link, the churched may suggest to their unchurched friends that they check out their church's website. Too often, however, websites are designed for those who already attend the church. They post the pastor's sermons, a calendar of meetings and events, and prayer lists of people. To someone unchurched, this is a list of people they don't know. The number of meetings might make them wonder if the church is heavy on administration and light on ministry. They don't know the pastor and may not be all that interested in what the pastor has to say.

Typically, websites are geared toward being information centers for members and not invitations to the unchurched. Like worship, we need to redirect our efforts toward invitational ministry and revamp our websites to be invitational and informational for the unchurched. For example, a common reason a person visits a church's website is to find out how much it costs to be married in the sanctuary. A church's website must make sure it informs users of the fees and the procedure for setting up a date for a wedding in the church's sanctuary or chapel. The website should indicate whether the church allows people who are not members to be married in its sanctuary and which pastor is available to offer pre-marriage counseling and to perform the wedding. Other users, especially the unchurched, may be wondering about the same information for baptisms and funerals, rituals the unchurched will show interest in. Many unchurched people are afraid that they cannot get married nor have their child baptized in the church if they are not members. Some churches don't allow this. Putting your church's policy on the website saves them from calling and being turned down.

The responsibility for the church's website and presence on Facebook and other sites ought to be given to one or more younger member(s) of the congregation who is more in tune with what other young people may be searching for. This is a great way to get the young people involved in the life of the church and to equip them to serve as invitational ministers for a new age.

Chapter 8

Creating a Culture of Invitation

"Our congregation is a different place today. We ourselves are different. No longer do we put our energy into making sure every little thing gets done so that the church is open for another Sunday; today, we offer opportunities for ministries. Members are a lot less interested in serving on a committee that does nothing but make decisions, and now want to learn how to be ministers.

"We were feeling in a rut; nothing ever changed—same ol', same ol' ever week. Thinking about any change made us feel so overwhelmed, we didn't make any. It was like we were looking through a keyhole and trying to stay focused on that while everything else around us was falling apart. Getting out of denial and facing reality was hard. Only then could we look at each other and admit that we weren't doing anything to help ourselves. How could we expect that God would be able to help us?

"Most of us knew that Jesus wanted us to make changes that would appeal to the young people. But how do you do that and not get the old people upset and angry? They are the life-blood of this church and their opinion should be held in high esteem. The lingering threat of losing a few people held us hostage from making the changes we needed to make to grow our congregation. We decided to follow Jesus."

"The thought of inviting someone to come to church had crossed my mind before. I felt so incompetent to do something like that. After my church had us all come to a workshop, we realized that everyone feels this way, because we didn't know what to say. I started with asking my adult children, and two out of three are now coming. That made me feel like "I can do this!" and so the other day I invited a woman I met at my knitting club. Before this all started, I would never have invited her."

129

"I was one of the people who wanted to vote (not build consensus) to close the church. If we can't get people to serve on committees, I thought, how on earth are we going to get all these teams to do all this work? I didn't think our church had it in them. Now that we have new families attending and people are excited about the future, I can witness that the miracle isn't what God does for us, it's what we have in ourselves to be able to do for God."

"OK. I'm embarrassed to tell you that we were the ones waiting for the bus of new people (LOL). When visitors came to the front door for the first time, we shook their hands, gave them bulletins, and showed them where to sit. That was being 'warm and friendly.' That was our evangelism program. Today, we invite them to the front door. It's a lot different. Something within us has changed."

"We couldn't figure out why young families weren't coming to our church any longer. Then we began walking around in our neighborhood. We noticed the rusty swing set in the park. We didn't see any children playing in a ball field covered in overgrown grass. We talked with a young mother in the grocery line. She told us that she was hoping to get enough money together to move to another neighborhood where there is a better school system for her children. We realized "young families" were not in our mission field and, if they were moving in, were looking for an opportunity to move out. We reached the decision that the best use of our money was to give it to a church that was reaching these young families."

"Our congregation is aging. Church is the one constant in my life. I don't want to learn to be an invitational minister. I just want a place to visit with my friends. I don't like change and I don't want it. I've had to attend the funerals of family members and friends and learn how to use a computer. The last thing I want is for someone to take away the one thing that hasn't changed on me. I don't want the church to close but I also know that that is what lies ahead for us."

"Our pastor used to be the one to do the ministry in this church. We thought he should be the one who also brought in new members. We thought that was in his job description. Now, he teaches us to do the ministry, and making disciples is our job. I feel so much better about myself, both as a person and as a member of a church. I feel more confident that I can make a difference in someone else's life and that feels good."

These voices of witness speak of the change that is necessary to create a culture of invitation. But change is not something that comes easily to religious organizations. A long and distinguished history, with traditions and rituals passed down from generation to generation, brings comfort and stability during times of loss, struggle, and suffering, but the idea of change seems to dishonor everything held to be sacrosanct. A congregation's identity, core values, and purpose are derived from and revolve around this history—a continuous history that unites us with all those who have gone before. We thrive on consistency and resist popular trends and short-lived cultural fads. Trying to decide when to let go of tradition and habit in favor of change is a difficult point to discern.

Culture has also changed more dramatically and rapidly than ever before. As culture changes to accommodate the social needs of the next generation, the church seems to be moving in slow motion—almost to counter-balance this movement—digging in its heels. Add to these cultural shifts the fact that so many congregations are comprised of individuals who have had to adapt to developmental changes such as retirement, loss of a spouse, or being forced to leave home and move to a place that provides nursing care. Too many are simply hoping that they can keep the church open long enough to have a place in which to hold their funeral.

Reflections on Change

The world around us is changing more rapidly and dramatically than perhaps ever before in its history. Technology has not only changed the way we communicate, but also the way we relate to one another. What feels less personal to one generation feels quite personal to another. Interpersonal communication used to be defined as two people present in the same room; today it may include two people on the Internet. To imagine that we could talk with someone on a phone that was not connected by a cord to a jack in the wall was beyond anyone's comprehension only a few years ago. Those in the generations that have experienced these changes have had to adapt. Even if the changes have had a positive impact upon our lives, something has had to change within us. Adapting to change takes energy. So does resisting change.

As change happens all around us, the church seems to have "adapted" by investing in keeping everything the same and resisting anything new and different. We have used much energy to sustain the status quo, probably at the expense of losing members who might have challenged us to look earlier at new ways of being church. For some congregations, so much energy devoted to resisting change has led to depression. Congregations wonder, "Who is going to do all of this work of putting together these invitational events?" They wonder if they have enough energy to go on. Instead of using up one's energy to resist the changes happening in our culture, perhaps we are better serving Jesus if we use that energy to adapt and learn new ways of being disciples to meet the spiritual needs of the next generation.

Instead of resisting change or investing in the status quo, congregations can create cultures that help individuals to better adapt to the change going on in the world around us. How do we, as an organization, help people to relate to each other, especially given the new advances in technology? How will text messaging impact the way that people form personal, intimate relationships with each other, in a time when even e-mail and talking on the cell phone are becoming passé? In what ways can religious organizations be the forerunners for other organizations to create a culture that embraces and embodies diversity, inviting all people of every age, race, and tongue into its culture to be both transformed by it as well as transformative of it?

In essence, invitational ministry invites people into a process of change. We will change the way we understand our relationship with God in Jesus, the way in which we will allow the Holy Spirit to work through us, and the way we understand ourselves and our purpose for Jesus' mission to the unchurched. We will change the way we view the church. Instead of it being an organization with a mission to take care of those inside of it, we will be outward-looking, focusing our gaze upon those who need us.

To navigate the process of change three targets of change come to mind. I have already written about the individual member and the congregation; now I will discuss the pastor. As the church is a system, changing one aspect of the system without changing the other two can prove counter-productive.[1] The system can either respond by moving in the opposite direction of change (slamming on the brakes) or it can slowly produce change. An organization only changes if the people who comprise that organization are the ones who are individually changing. So many denominations today are paying lip service to "changing lives," and yet I am not quite sure in what way they can claim this new mantra of "purpose."

The Pastor

Thus far, I have had little to say about the role of the pastor in the process of making-disciples. The reason for my silence has been to deemphasize the idea that the pastor is the one who is supposed to bring in new people. As long as he or she is solely responsible for invitational ministry, churches will experience significant decline. For one thing, pastors do not tend to have the same opportunities for interaction outside the church as members do (for example, colleagues at work, interest groups). Additionally, only one person inviting from one church will probably only bring in a trickle of people, whereas if every member is inviting, there will be a lot more people becoming disciples. Third, church members, as well as the pastor, have a spiritual need to do work that is meaningful and purposeful.

Change in the culture of a congregation tends to be pastor-driven. The pastor functions as the mover and shaker of the change and tries to convince the members that this change is in their best interests. He or she has to invest energy into convincing, energy that may be better used to equip members for ministry. The process often unfolds this way: the pastor thinks of the idea, plans out how to go about implementing the idea, considers who may be willing to implement the idea (sometimes instead of who has the skill), and then asks that person or persons. Pastors often complain about having so much to do. They speak of being overworked. Their over-functioning, however, has contributed to the numerical decline in our congregations. The more ministry they do, the fewer opportunities there are for the disciples to do ministry. Today, the unchurched want to do ministry, not watch ordained ministers spin frantically, soloing in their skill and unraveling from the stress.

Some pastors, consciously or unconsciously, sabotage change because they themselves are resistant. They know that change accompanies conflict and they themselves feel ill-equipped to deal with conflict. Many pastors have had to handle a conflict situation in the past, one that they did not handle well, and so they invest their energy in suppressing conflict, during which time the need for change also gets suppressed. The pastor assumes that as long as he or she does what is expected, does not make any change to the worship service, and does pastoral visitation, then conflict will not arise. For the pastor who is close to retirement, he or she may be functioning on cruise control and not want to start something that he or she cannot finish. Nothing new begins. Members become bored and put their energy into the management of the organization. Decline sets in.

There is no bus of new people on the way to the front door. Members need to board the bus to go out into the community and invite a new generation of believers to come to the church so that they can learn anew for ministry. The pastor will be the one who drives the bus, but only for as long as necessary while he or she trains someone else to drive. (Congregations that have to convince the pastor to get on the bus often become frustrated when the pastor tries to give directions from the back seat.) The pastors who have taught others to drive witness that equipping members for ministry has freed up their time to be able to pursue other interests—such as a doctorate of ministry degrees, the stacks of reading sitting on their desks, or exploring their own spiritual yearnings.

The Discipleship Model of Congregational Culture

For the past fifty years, the membership model has served the mainline church well. Its focus met the needs of that generation: learning about God and offering events in which people new to the suburbs could develop social friendships. People selected a church based on denominational affiliation, joined to meet a need to belong, and participated by attending weekly worship and activities and committee meetings. Organizational needs defined ministries that were centered upon those who were churched. The structure of the church remained relatively consistent and tradition trumped innovation. During times when everyone belonged to a church a membership model was the best choice for a congregation's culture. But during times when most people don't go to church, a membership model will not sustain the life of a congregation and will be counter-productive to reaching those who are unchurched.

To create a culture of invitation that seeks to bring into the church another generation of believers, we need a different model, one that better reflects the spiritual needs of another generation. Such a model is emerging in congregations practicing invitational ministry. I call this "the discipleship model," as I am advocating for a shift from referring to "members" of a congregation to "disciples," and their relationship with one another as "brothers and sisters in Christ" rather than "friends." This model supports the efforts to equip members to become disciples by inviting people to participate in a religious organization in new and different ways than have been customary in the membership model.

In the discipleship model, people come to the church because someone else invited them. They do not need to "belong," and the boundary line between who is in and who is out is less well-defined. People do not join, and there is no ritual of joining. Attendance at worship is expected as well as small group faith sharing, mission projects, and invitational events. The focus is on experiencing God *and* talking about those experiences to form faith. Individual passions determine what the organization has to offer to equip people for ministry. The structure and by-laws are designed to be in line with the vision statement of "who we believe that God is calling us to become as a congregation." Innovation trumps tradition when that tradition is no longer relevant. Individual identity defines the organization. (For example, "I am spiritual but not religious and looking for an organization to engage in with others who define themselves this way.")

In the membership model, most people visit the church by attending a worship service. In the discipleship model, they come because someone invited them to an event. Programs, activities, worship, interest groups, and liturgical arts are all points of entry into congregational life. People will not come because they feel obligated, but because they are hopeful that organized religion has something to offer to them. Unlike membership classes that teach new members what they need to know to function like the current members, discipleship classes prepare people for ministry. In the discipleship model, congregational culture is constantly changing because just when we figure out how to meet the needs of one generation, we have to reinvent ourselves all over again to meet the needs of the next generation.

Transitioning from the Membership Model to the Discipleship Model

"It's so exciting to see so many new people coming to our church!" That's the kind of statement heard in a congregation when the vision has become reality. For a congregation that has experienced decline for many years, seeing new people attend events and worship creates new energy and enthusiasm. After a long time of depression, with frequent dips into the pool of despair, the presence of new people is greeted with a long-awaited joyful spirit. The congregation's mood is now one of celebration. Members feel differently about these new people because they invited them (versus new people showing up at the front door). So part of their excitement reflects feeling affirmed for their invitational ministry skills. Members turn to one another and witness, "Wow, we really can do this!" The congregation is numerically growing because of their efforts, not because of outside cultural factors. Even if they began this transition with the goal to save the organization, they begin to realize that something has changed within themselves as individuals. They are more aware that the Holy Spirit is working through them to practice invitational ministry.

But Jesus says that discipleship *costs* (Mt. 16:24–26). When we can anticipate these costs, we are better prepared to help people adapt to their changing reality. Things will never again be the same. The organization is changing just by the presence of new people. Members may now want the new people to function under the membership model, but the membership model will not hold up this new house. Time and time again, congregations have made select changes to numerically grow, but not changed their culture to sustain that growth, and then watched helplessly as the numbers declined again–often below the beginning level. Declining momentum tends to take others with it, which explains why so many churched people become inactive. Leaders need to be prepared for moments of regret during this transitioning process, from both the churched and the new people. Members had imagined what it would be like to have "all these new people," and, while this initially generates excitement, that feeling is likely to subside. The membership model will insist that the new people assimilate to "the way we do things" and even the best-intentioned members will find themselves defending that model. There will be a regressive pull like a magnet to function with the membership model (even if they call it something different) because when people get anxious they want to return to a time of functioning when they recall feeling less anxious. They had anticipated that numerical church growth would alleviate their anxiety (and solve all their problems), only to now realize that they are anxious about other things and have encountered a new set of problems.

Similarly, new people are often so excited about their new church. They will invite others who will be drawn to attending because they sense this excitement. They love the people and the pastor and project a positive picture of the congregation's culture. Individuals who have recently made a decision to do something usually look for cues in their environment to affirm that they made a good decision. This dynamic, which is often subconscious or unconscious, serves to blind them to glaring problems and potential deal-breakers. For the immediate moment, they are content to be part of an organization that uses the membership model because they are unaware of anything different. In time, however, they too will transition to seeing things that they think need to change in order to hold their interest. They too will reach a critical point when they perceive that the congregation's culture needs to change.

New people come with new ideas. They can often see things that members cannot see or that members don't want to see. They will sense the anxiety and not understand what it is about. They may have little or no emotional investment in returning to the way things have always been because they weren't there; that's not "going home" for them. When they see things that they think should change, they don't understand why everyone else doesn't see them. "I don't get it. If that isn't working, why don't we change it?" With no background or history of why that change was made in the first place, they may get easily frustrated that the congregation seems so unwilling to change. The force with which the need for change is presented by a new person may have a counter-effect; members may become even more committed to "the way we do things" to preserve the esteem of the organization.

The motivation for why a congregation reaches out to its community may be revisited during this part of the process. If the new people were invited to solve money problems, they will probably figure this out during their first few months in the church. Congregations that reach out to numerically grow a congregation for reasons that are not theological are often unwilling to make changes that are needed to make it easy for the new people to continue to come. They tend to be the most resistant because what they wanted was to have enough money to continue to function as the same kind of church they have always been. It will become evident at this time why the congregation needed to spend much prayerful time in discerning why Jesus was calling them to reach out to the new people. Those who passed over this part of the process will find that they struggle to keep the new people interested in coming.

New people come with new ideas based on their own spiritual needs. In the membership model, new people were churched elsewhere and so they came with spiritual needs similar or aligned with the spiritual needs of those who were already churched there. Now, instead of insisting that newcomers adapt and adjust to the status quo, a congregation will need to be receptive to their ideas. That doesn't necessarily mean the organization will make every change suggested by every new person. The congregation that is willing to experiment with changes will find that some of the new ideas actually benefit everyone, and there will be some churched people whose spiritual needs are met by the changes. Congregations who present changes as experiments that will later be evaluated find that as long as people have a forum to voice their opinions, they are more willing to try new things. Only when congregations think that changes will be etched in stone for all eternity do they become resistant.

God parted the Red Sea and Moses led the Israelites out of Egypt and into the wilderness. When they became anxious about not knowing what would become of them, the Israelites wanted to return to the land of the familiar. Congregations experiencing numerical growth, an indicator that they are practicing invitational ministry, will have moments of wanting to go back to "the way we have always done things." Pastors may remind people that they could not continue the way they were going (not reaching out to their neighborhood), that their discomfort has brought them this far and that, with prayer, they will continue to move closer to

God. As long as members and new people alike discern that "this is what God wants for our church," they will be able to navigate through the wilderness and move closer to the Promised Land.

One thing is abundantly clear: a church cannot go back. Once a congregation begins inviting new people, they cannot decide that the new people are no longer welcome. You can't uninvite them! Congregations that are moving in the direction of becoming multicultural should consider that when people of diverse backgrounds begin attending, the congregation will never again be segregated. This is a good thing. There will be moments when the regret is associated with diversity. In my own experience as pastor of a multicultural congregation, those moments of regret are short-lived. People come to appreciate the rich diversity of traditions, music, and perspective as valuable to the life of a congregation.

Leaders should anticipate that members will need to grieve that what they expected it would be like to have new people and what they expected to gain may not be happening. If they hoped for money, they may be disappointed that the new people do not contribute as much as those who are long-term members. Small groups of faith-sharing or skills-learning need to be in place because members will express the loss of the family feeling they formerly felt in worship. These small groups will provide another type of opportunity for that level of intimacy. The invitational team may need to provide opportunities for members to express sadness that their beloved church is changing by the mere presence of new people. They need to have a safe place to express these feelings so that they do not interfere with the process of making disciples of the new people. If newcomers sense that their presence in the congregation is making the members feel sad, they are not likely to keep coming. Eventually, if the team gives members a chance to grieve about what once was and what they had expected would come to be, the joy of having new members will overcome the sadness.

Without acknowledging these feelings, the organization risks becoming emotionally unhealthy. Members may begin to blame the newcomers for their own feelings of sadness and loss. Signs that this may be happening should be continually assessed. For instance, a member may call the pastor for care and be told that the pastor isn't available. Before the new people arrived, that member trusted that if the pastor wasn't available, he or she must be busy with something else of equal importance. When new people start coming, the same member may become angry when the pastor is unavailable. "I've been a member of this church my entire life, and when I need the pastor, the pastor should be there for me!" This member may jump to the conclusion that the pastor is too busy providing care to one of the new people. Members often think that the pastor pays more attention to new people than to the current members.

Likewise, new people will have second thoughts about participating in a religious organization. Invitational ministers have helped them to have interest in the church, yet now the hard part comes when the congregation is faced with making the changes that are needed to meet their spiritual needs. Whereas a few months ago they loved everything about their new church, they now begin to note that the worship seems to drag a little in places. They may have attended worship every week, but the first few Sundays had praise bands and alternative music that has been replaced with organ music. They may realize that the congregation planned special Sundays for the first few weeks that they would be invited to worship, but has now returned to the regular style of worship. The pastor who was so attentive the first couple of weeks may not remember their names. They are now being asked to financially contribute to the organization. Things have changed.

They can keep these ideas to themselves and invest in the status quo. They are often willing to do this because they like the people who attend the church and don't want to hurt their feelings. They may feel that suggesting something different is accusing the current members of doing things wrong, and they don't want to put their new church sisters and brothers on the defensive. With time, they may begin to think like someone who is churched and less like someone who is unchurched. Most organizations naturally function to encourage a kind of group think to maintain the status quo (not necessarily a healthy dynamic). When we ask newcomers to help us keep the organization functioning in the same way, we have regressed back to an inward focus. If newcomers go with the flow and accept the status quo, but remain ambivalent, the church will risk losing them. Often new people are figuring out what the status quo is so as not to challenge it. They want to fit in like everyone else. If no one else seems to think that something is a problem, then they will think they are the only one with this concern. If so, they are likely to stop attending.

The discipleship model of creating a culture of invitation within a congregation means that everyone's spiritual needs are of equal importance. Newcomers are integrated into the life of the congregation with the same respect and value as the other servants.

Conclusion

Jesus says, "Love thy neighbor as thyself." When congregations experience decline, they struggle to love themselves. Everyone has worked diligently to do everything possible to attract another generation, and yet they are not coming. Every week, members observe that there are fewer people in attendance than the week before. Depression hovers as the church seems to be moving closer to the edge of the cliff. Members fear that if something doesn't change soon, their beloved church will succumb to financial pressures and close. But it doesn't have to be this way. A congregation can choose to give its money to another congregation that is reaching out to "love thy neighbor" so that monies go to their intended use: to support the ministries that are reaching another generation. A congregation that believes that God wants them to do a turnaround can do one. Every congregation that feels called to numerically grow can do so.

We can't love our neighbors if we don't know them. A turnaround is only possible when a congregation works toward reconnecting with their neighborhood in such a way that conveys that the church cares about its neighbors. Therefore, the congregation has to become aware of the issues that its neighbors are struggling with—the conversation among the "spiritual but not religious" crowd, their joys and concerns. What kinds of activities, programs, and events would help them? What does the church have to offer the unchurched to help form their faith? I have suggested that the church needs to offer entry points other than worship to help our neighbors also get to know us.

Invitational ministry helps us to put love into practice. As we more fully love our neighbor, and as we increase our concern about their spiritual formation, we more fully love ourselves. As members of the congregational transition to become invitational ministers, their lives will be changed. With hope, we move forward to equip another generation to continue the ministry and mission that Christ calls us to.

Notes

Chapter 1: The Christian Practice of Invitational Ministry

1   See Carol Howard Merritt, *Reframing Hope: Vital Ministry in a New Generation* (Herndon, Va.: Alban, 2010).

2   Diana Butler Bass refers to Christian practices in many of her writings. A good introduction can be found in *The Practicing Congregation: Imagining a New Old Church* (Herndon, Va.: Alban, 2004). She goes into more detail about these practices in id., *From Nomads to Pilgrims: Stories from Practicing Congregations* (Herndon, Va.: Alban, 2006). See also id.,, *Christianity for the Rest of Us: How the Neighborhood Church Is Transforming the Faith* (San Francisco: HarperOne, 2006).

3   See Robert Putman, *Bowling Alone: The Collapse and Revival of American Community* (New York: Simon & Schuster, 2000).

4   Phyllis Tickle, *The Great Emergence: How Christianity Is Changing and Why* (Grand Rapids, Mich.: Baker Books, reprint 2012).

5   The first out of the four books in the series used for small group discussion is Martha Grace Reese, *Unbinding the Gospel: Real Life Evangelism* (St. Louis: Chalice Press, 2008). The other titles are: *Unbinding Your Heart, Unbinding Your Church,* and *Unbinding Your Soul.*

6   Laurene Beth Bowers, *Designing Contemporary Congregations* (Cleveland: Pilgrim Press, 2008).

Chapter 2: Why Practice Invitational Worship?

1   Medium-size churches that have decreased in membership still function as if they are medium-size, thus demanding more energy from their membership.

2   A 1960 American film written by Charles B. Griffith about a plant that feeds on human flesh and constantly demands to be fed. Source: Wikipedia, http://en.wikipedia.org/wiki/The_Little_Shop_of_Horrors.

Chapter 3: The Mission Field

1   David Kinnaman, *You Lost Me: Why Young Christians Are Leaving Church...and Rethinking Faith* (Grand Rapids, Mich.: Baker Books, 2011), 171ff.

2   The two that I use are Percept and Mission Insite.

Chapter 5: Planning Invitational Events

1   See Laurene Beth Bowers, *Becoming a Multicultural Church* (Cleveland: Pilgrim Press, 2006).

Chapter 6: Framing Invitations

1   Diana Butler Bass, *Christianity after Religion: The End of Church and the Birth of a New Spiritual Awakening* (New York: HarperOne, 2012).

Chapter 8: Creating a Culture of Invitation

1   Several authors have written about Systems Theory, such as Murray Bowen in *Family Theory in Clinical Practice,* rev. ed. (New York: Jason Aronson, 1993), and Edwin Friedman in *Generation to Generation: Family Process in Church and Synagogue* (New York: Guilford Press, 1985).